LIFE LESSONS

— *from* —

JESUS

LIFE LESSONS

— *from* —

JESUS

36 BIBLE STUDIES
for Individuals or Groups

Bill Hybels
AND John Ortberg

WITH KEVIN *and* SHERRY HARNEY

 ZONDERVAN®
.com

 WILLOW
Willow Creek Resources

ZONDERVAN

Life Lessons from Jesus

This title is also available as a Zondervan ebook. Visit www.zondervan.com/ebooks.

The Lord's Prayer: Praying with Power by John Ortberg
Copyright © 2008 by Willow Creek Association

Luke: Lessons from Jesus by Bill Hybels
Copyright © 2008 by Willow Creek Association

Parables: Imagine Life God's Way by John Ortberg
Copyright © 2002 by Willow Creek Association

The Passion Story: Uphill Faith by Bill Hybels
Copyright © 2009 by Willow Creek Association

Sermon on the Mount 1: Connect with God by Bill Hybels
Copyright © 2002 by Willow Creek Association

Sermon on the Mount 2: Connect with God by Bill Hybels
Copyright © 2002 by Willow Creek Association

Requests for information should be addressed to:

Zondervan, 3900 *Sparks Dr. SE, Grand Rapids, Michigan 49546*

ISBN 978-0-310-82002-4

All Scripture quotations, unless otherwise indicated, are taken from The Holy Bible, *New Interna-tional Version®, NIV®*. Copyright © 1973, 1978, 1984, 2011 by Biblica, Inc.® Used by permission. All rights reserved worldwide.

Scripture quotations marked NASB are taken from the *New American Standard Bible*. Copyright © 1960, 1962, 1963, 1968, 1971, 1972, 1973, 1975, 1977, 1995 by The Lockman Foundation. Used by permission.

Any Internet addresses (websites, blogs, etc.) and telephone numbers in this book are offered as a resource. They are not intended in any way to be or imply an endorsement by Zondervan, nor does Zondervan vouch for the content of these sites and numbers for the life of this book.

All rights reserved. No part of this publication may be reproduced, stored in a retrieval system, or trans-mitted in any form or by any means — electronic, mechanical, photocopy, recording, or any other — except for brief quotations in printed reviews, without the prior permission of the publisher.

Cover design: Faceout Studio
Cover photography: Shutterstock®
Interior photography: Shutterstock®
Interior design: Beth Shagene

First printing May 2014 / Printed in the United States of America

Contents

THE PARABLES OF JESUS

THE PRACTICES OF JESUS

THE PASSION OF JESUS

How to Use This Study

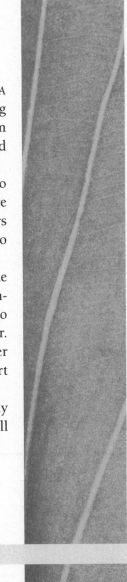

IMAGINE THAT YOU WERE ONE OF THE DISCIPLES SITTING AT JESUS' FEET ON A Galilean hillside, walking beside him on the dusty Judean roads, reclining with him at the dinner table. What would it have been like to hear him teach, or to see him heal leprous skin, challenge the religious leaders, and calm stormy waters?

What lessons did these first-century followers learn from the One who often said, "Whoever has ears, let them hear," and once asked, "Do you have eyes but fail to see?" And what lessons do we twenty-first century followers learn from the accounts that some of those same disciples committed to memory and then to the written word?

If we're completely honest, we've become so overly familiar with some of Jesus' teachings that we're no longer amazed or affected by them. Others, we've never been very comfortable with—they seem too radical, too demanding. And maybe there are still others that we've forgotten altogether.

Perhaps it's time for a "refresher course"—to sit again at the Master Teacher's feet, to fall in love once more with the One who wooed your heart and soul, to become a disciple not just in name but in practice.

In these thirty-six sessions drawn from the bestselling New Community series, respected Bible teachers and authors Bill Hybels and John Ortberg will guide you through life-changing lessons from the Gospels as you explore:

- The perspectives of Jesus
- The prayer of Jesus
- The principles of Jesus
- The parables of Jesus
- The practices of Jesus
- The passion of Jesus

About This Workbook

To get the most from this study you need to understand a few basic facts:

- It is designed to be flexible. You can use it in your individual quiet times or for group discussion (small groups, neighborhood Bible studies, etc.).
- Each of the thirty-six studies typically focuses on only one or two passages. That allows you to see each passage in its context, avoiding the temptation of proof texting and the frustration of "Bible hopscotch" (jumping from verse to verse). If you would like to look up additional passages, a Bible concordance will give the most help.

- Each study follows the same basic structure: a short introduction; "Making the Connection" (an entry question to the lesson topic); "Knowing and Being Known" (Bible readings and reflection/discussion questions); "Celebrating and Being Celebrated" (prayer suggestions); and "Loving and Being Loved" and "Serving and Being Served" (application ideas). "Resource boxes" are also interspersed among the reflection/discussion questions to enrich your time in God's Word or add further insight on the topic.

- The questions help you *discover* what the Bible says rather than simply *telling* you what it says. They encourage you to think and to explore options rather than to merely fill in the blanks with one-word answers.

Suggestions for Individual Study

1. Begin each study with prayer. Ask God to help you understand the passage and apply it to your life.

2. A good modern translation, such as the *New International Version*, the *English Standard Version*, or the *New Living Translation*, will give you the most help. However, the questions in this guide are based on the *New International Version*.

3. Read and reread the passage(s). You must know what the passage says before you can understand what it means and how it applies to you.

4. Write your answers in the space provided. This will help you to clearly express your understanding of the passage.

5. Keep a Bible dictionary handy. Use it to look up any unfamiliar words, names, or places.

Suggestions for Group Study

1. Come to the study prepared. Careful preparation will greatly enrich your time in group discussion.

2. Be willing to join in the discussion or to encourage discussion if you are leading the group. Plan to share what God has taught you in your individual study.

3. Stick to the passage being studied. Base your answers on the verses being discussed rather than on outside authorities such as commentaries or your favorite author or speaker.

4. Try to be sensitive to the other members of the group. Listen attentively when they speak, and be affirming whenever you can. This will encourage more hesitant members of the group to participate.

5. Be careful not to dominate the discussion. By all means, participate! But allow others to have equal time.

THE PERSPECTIVES *of* JESUS

Bill Hybels

The Beatitudes

Part 1

MATTHEW 5:1 – 12

JESUS HAD A UNIQUE WAY OF CHALLENGING PEOPLE'S THINKING AND GIVING them new perspectives as they looked at the world. When you read through the life of Jesus, you will discover that he often helped to open eyes that were shut ... both literally and metaphorically.

To those who looked at themselves and were proud of the fact that they had never murdered anyone, Jesus told them to look a little closer. He wanted them to see the anger in their hearts and to recognize that their words could be like an arrow aimed at an unsuspecting heart.

To those who were persecuted and hurting, he helped them see that there could be blessing in the midst of pain. He told them to look deeper and to see the other side of pain and realize that God could use it to bring heavenly blessings into their lives.

The disciples saw the little children coming to Jesus and wanted to keep them from distracting Jesus from the important ministry he was doing. Jesus helped his followers see that these children were the heirs of the kingdom of heaven. They were not a distraction from his ministry; they were objects of his affection.

The religious leaders looked across the landscape and saw it littered with undesirables such as tax collectors, prostitutes, lepers, and sinners. Jesus saw these people and invited them as honored guests to the banquet his Father was preparing for all who would follow the Son of God.

From the day he began his public ministry, Jesus has been about the business of opening closed eyes and changing the way people see the world. This was true two thousand years ago and it is just as true today!

Making the Connection

1. Tell about how your relationship with Jesus has changed the way you see *one* of the following. (NOTE: When you see questions with checkmark options throughout this workbook, simply checkmark the box you choose to answer, and then write your reply in the space provided.)

   ☐ People who are outcast and rejected in our society

   ☐ People who have hurt you and wronged you

   ☐ The value and importance of material things

   ☐ Who you are and your value in this world

Knowing and Being Known

Read Matthew 5:1 – 12

2. As you read these nine beatitudes, what do you learn about how God wants us to relate to others?

Blessed Are Those Who Mourn

Jesus offers a wave of tender consolation for all those who are bent over with sorrow. For years when I read this beatitude I thought Jesus was calling people to a consistent condition of mourning ... as if he was saying that if we would spend more time sorrowing, we would find more blessedness. Yet this seems to contradict other straightforward passages in the Bible that promise that those who follow Christ will live with a deep sense of inner joy, confidence, hope, and freedom!

So what is Jesus trying to say? The answer is found in the second part of this beatitude. Jesus is saying that those who are overcome with sorrow and sadness find a special blessing as God draws near to them in their time of need. Jesus is saying that he knows we can be overwhelmed by sorrow, we can feel that we are fighting a losing battle with tears at every turn, yet he has good news for us. For those who feel there is no comfort for them Jesus is saying, "I have good news for you!" In his kingdom we will find comfort. In what can feel like a cold and harsh universe, consolation is found in him!

Read Matthew 5:4 and 2 Corinthians 1:3 – 4

3. What is the relationship between our times of mourning and God's commitment to extend comfort to us?

What is the relationship between our times of mourning and our ability to extend comfort to others when they are hurting?

4. Tell about a time when you experienced sorrow and mourning. How did you receive the comfort of God in *one* of the following ways?

☐ Through the touch and presence of the Holy Spirit

☐ Through God using the love and care of another follower of Christ

☐ Through the truth you learned from the Bible

☐ In some other way

5. Describe a time when God used you to extend compassion and comfort to a person who was in a time of sorrow and mourning. How did you feel when you realized God was ministering his comfort through you?

Blessed Are the Meek

In every crowd there are people who don't push and shove to get to the front of the line. They don't step on others to get to the top of the pile in the workplace. They don't read books on winning through intimidation. And they would never take twenty-five items through a ten-items-or-less line at the supermarket. These folks have a genuinely gentle heart and a meek spirit.

Over time these people learn that they don't usually do well in highly competitive, performance-oriented settings or systems, even religious systems. Instead, they get out of the way and let the achievers and thrivers beat each other up on their way to the top. Lots of times, if the truth be known, these humble and gentle types even secretly beat themselves up because of the way they are. They have heard parents who warned, "Come on, you can't just sit there and let the world come to you. Get out there and compete, scrape, claw, work hard, and do unto others before they do unto you!" They have heard teachers and speakers say, "Get out there and take on the world. If you can conceive it, you can achieve it!" There are days when these gentle-spirited people wonder if they were accidentally placed on the wrong planet.

In this beatitude, Jesus looked to the back of the crowd where the meek would have been sitting — after all, the meek would never have pushed their way in to get the good seats near the front! — and spoke directly to them. He wanted them to know the good news that the kingdom of God is open to them. And he wanted them to know that they would not have to scrape, claw, compete, or step on people to get in!

Read Matthew 5:5

6. In the economy of *this world*, who is it that will inherit the earth and all of its fullness? How is the teaching of Jesus in this beatitude radically countercultural?

7. When you hear Jesus speak of the meek and gentle among us, who comes to your mind, and what is it about that person's life that you would most like to emulate?

Blessed Are the Merciful

Jesus wants us to know that merciful people will not be marginalized in his kingdom. In the society of his day, no one paid much attention to mercy-givers. They were not the heroes of the society. In case you wonder if our society is much different, ask yourself when was the last time you saw the picture of an outrageous mercy-giver on the cover of a national news magazine? Does *Forbes* magazine tabulate and publicize the exploits and accomplishments of America's 100 most merciful people? Do TV shows celebrate "Lifestyles of the Kind and Merciful"? Do colleges offer scholarships to the most merciful and compassionate students graduating from high school?

Jesus says that God himself will give special attention to those who have shown mercy. They will not run out of mercy energy, because God will refill their mercy tanks with his own heart of mercy. God has a special place in his heart for the merciful on this earth because they are showing his mercy in a mercy-starved world.

Read Matthew 5:7

8. Why is it so important for mercy-givers to have their mercy tanks refueled and filled up by God?

What would happen to these people if they never received fresh fillings of God's mercy?

9. In what way could you extend mercy to a mercy-giver you know? How could you be God's vehicle to help refuel his mercy tank so that he can continue his ministry to others?

Blessed Are the Peacemakers

What does it mean to say that those who seek peace and make peace will be called "sons of God"? Isn't there only one Son of God — Jesus? Well, yes. But we need to remember that Jesus was sent to this earth to make peace. He is called the Prince of Peace. He came to reconcile us to the Father and to each other. He wants to make peace between wayward, selfish sinners and a holy God. Christ was the ultimate peacemaker, the cosmic reconciler.

Once we are restored to God through Christ, we receive a ministry of reconciliation. The Holy Spirit works in us and motivates us to put an end to all the battles and wars going on in our relational world. He wants us at peace with friends, spouses, children, parents, coworkers, church members, and neighbors. His people are called to be about the work of seeking peace and tearing down the walls that divide.

Read Matthew 5:9 and Colossians 1:17 – 20

10. Jesus Christ, the Son of God, is the ultimate peacemaker. What has Jesus done to make peace between us and the Father?

What has he done and what is he doing to help us make peace with each other?

11. What are some of the things we can do to be peacemakers in *one* of the following places?

☐ In our homes   ☐ In our community

☐ In our churches   ☐ In our world

Celebrating and Being Celebrated

Lift up prayers of thanksgiving and praise to God for extending his wonderful comfort to you during times you have experienced loss, mourning, and sorrow.

Loving and Being Loved

Often the meek among us, even in the church, are not noticed or affirmed for who they are. Yet these gentle and meek-spirited people add so much to the church and the lives of those around them. Identify one or two meek-spirited people that you know. Commit to finding some practical way to affirm and bless these people for their life and ministry. Let them know that you see the heart of Christ in them and that their gentle spirit inspires you to be more like Jesus.

Serving and Being Served

We all face times of mourning and sorrow. During these times we need brothers and sisters in Christ who will come alongside us and extend support and encouragement. Identify a person you know who has gone, or is going, through a time of loss. Find one practical way you can serve this person and help lift the load he or she is carrying at this time.

The Beatitudes

Part 2

MATTHEW 5:1 – 12

SOME TIME AGO I HAD A CHANCE TO SIT AT A DINNER TABLE WITH AN INDY race car driver. Throughout the meal I could not help but begin asking questions about what it is like to drive one of these powerful cars. I asked what it is like to drive over 250 mph down the backstretch of a raceway. What does it feel like to pass someone going 230 mph and to come within inches of their car or feel the buzz and smell the burn of tires on tires? What is it like to get loose in a turn going 190 mph? I just kept asking the questions and he kept giving me answers. He loved talking about it. You might say I sat there in wide-eyed wonderment during the course of that meal. I was taking in everything he said.

Some years ago I spoke with an astronaut. This guy had actually spent time on the moon! When we would sit down for meals together, I found myself amazed at what this man had experienced. It was so strange and foreign to me that I just took in every word he said. I asked him about what it felt like to be weightless. *What did the earth look like when you were standing on the moon? Did you ever get sick of Tang?* I sat in wide-eyed wonderment in this situation as well.

Do you know what wide-eyed wonderment is? It is when you are thoroughly fascinated with the subject matter and you can't seem to take it all in. This happens when you begin to hear about something so new, so strange, or so foreign to your life experience that you are staggered by what you hear. I believe this is what the crowd must have felt when Jesus sat on the mountainside and taught about his kingdom. It was all so new, so powerful, and so fresh that they must have been in complete wide-eyed wonderment.

Making the Connection

1. Describe a situation in which you found yourself in wide-eyed wonderment.

   Tell about a *spiritual* experience that left you in wide-eyed wonderment.

Knowing and Being Known

Read Matthew 5:1 – 12

2. Which of these words of blessing (beatitudes) speaks to our relationship with God and which ones speak to our relationship with each other?

   How do some of these beatitudes speak to both our relationship with God and each other?

3. Each of the beatitudes has two parts: part one begins, "Blessed are ..." and part two begins "for they ..." The second part of each of these beatitudes grows out of the first part. Some of the beatitudes seem to make sense and fit into our worldview; others do not. Identify one of the beatitudes that makes sense to you (in other words, one in which you think that part two grows naturally out of part one). Explain what you believe Jesus is communicating in this beatitude and why it makes sense to you.

4. Some of the beatitudes seem almost backwards. Identify one of the beatitudes that does not seem to make sense (in other words, part two does *not* seem to grow naturally out of part one). What do you think Jesus is trying to communicate through this seemingly backward statement?

Blessed Are the Poor in Spirit

The scribes and Pharisees in the crowd that day were wealthy in spiritual knowledge and piety, and downright affluent in spiritual activities. They were raising the spiritual bar higher and higher and were certain they could leap over it in a single bound! They did not need anything from Jesus. They had manufactured enough righteousness in their own human willpower that they could say, "We don't need what you are talking about. We are rich in spirit."

There was another group in the crowd that day. These were the poor in spirit. This group knew they were not members of the spiritual honor society. They knew they were not setting righteousness records. They would freely admit that they were not impressive spiritually, morally, or ethically. In fact, people in that group hung their heads low because they knew their spiritual net worth was downright scandalous.

5. Like the scribes and Pharisees of the first century, we can be tempted to think we are "rich in spirit." What are some signals or signs that spiritual pride is creeping in and that a person is beginning to believe he or she is rich in spirit?

Why is spiritual pride such a dangerous heart condition?

6. Describe a time when you were deeply struck by your poverty of spirit.

How did this reality draw you closer to the heart of God?

Blessed Are Those Who Hunger and Thirst for Righteousness

There is a miraculous transfer at the heart of biblical Christianity. Theologians call it "imputed righteousness." This spiritual reality sets Christianity apart from every other religion in the world.

In every other religious system, a person finds righteousness through following a set of religious rules and regulations. The more you follow the rules, the more righteousness you find. In Christianity, we experience imputed righteousness. It is *given* to us by God, not *earned*. When we realize that we have insufficient righteousness in our heart and life and come to the point where we know we will never measure up or achieve God's standard of perfect righteousness, we have taken the first step. At this point we begin to hunger and thirst for the righteousness we can never find on our own. Finally, we look heavenward and cry, "I want to be in a right relationship with you, God, but I know there is no way I can do it! Help me, God!"

In that moment, God hears our cry and orders the transfer of the righteousness of Jesus Christ to our account. We are made righteous because of Christ, not by anything we have done. His righteousness is imputed to us, and on that final day, when we stand before the Father, we will be seen as perfectly righteous because of what God has done for us through his Son, Jesus.

Read 2 Corinthians 5:21 and 1 John 4:9 – 10

7. What is the role of God the Father in imputed righteousness?

What is the role of God the Son in this process?

8. What spiritual realities or life experiences have caused you to hunger and thirst for God's righteousness?

What can we do as followers of Christ to deepen our hunger for the things of God?

Blessed Are the Pure in Heart

Jesus declared over and over again that God pays more attention to internals than externals. This was a slap in the face of the entire superficial system of spirituality set up by the scribes and Pharisees of Jesus' day. Jesus was emphasizing issues of the heart, while the scribes and Pharisees insisted that proof of your spiritual pudding was found in how many of the external rules you kept. In effect, these religious professionals were acting as spiritual scorekeepers. They were saying, "We will let you know how you are doing. If you follow all the rules and regulations, no one will ever ask any questions about what is going on inside of you."

Jesus' message was radically different! He was saying, "Look deep down inside your heart. Is internal transformation happening? Is your heart growing more and more pure?" For Jesus, growth in purity was the true sign of spiritual authenticity.

9. From kindergarten to the end of our lives, this world drives us to focus on externals. What are some examples of how our culture places a primary value on externals?

What are some examples of how this mind-set has invaded the church?

10. What are some disciplines and practices that can help a follower of Christ grow in purity?

What is one goal you want to set for your personal growth in purity, and how might fellow believers pray for you and encourage you to grow in this area of your spiritual life?

Celebrating and Being Celebrated

Consider at least five qualities or attributes of God that lead you to wide-eyed wonderment:

1.

2.

3.

4.

5.

Then celebrate these wonderful qualities and attributes in prayer.

Loving and Being Loved

Take time this week to express your love to the One who loves you most, your heavenly Father. Write a letter to God, expressing the depth of your appreciation for his grace that is revealed perfectly in Jesus Christ. Thank him for extending grace rather than setting up a complex religious system filled with rules and regulations.

Serving and Being Served

Your desire to serve others grows out of the knowledge that God has served you beyond what you could ever deserve. Commit to memorize 1 John 4:9–10 in the coming week. Rejoice in the righteousness of Christ you have received through Jesus' death on the cross and his resurrection.

Being Salt and Light

MATTHEW 5:13 – 16

JESUS IS DEEPLY CONCERNED ABOUT HOW WE RELATE TO OTHERS IN THE FAMILY of God. He is also profoundly committed to teaching us how we are to be in relationship with those who are not yet his followers. Lost people matter to him. In teaching us about our relationship with those outside of the family, Jesus uses two vivid word pictures: He says that we are to be *salt* and *light*. In the opening verses of this chapter, Jesus says that the most persuasive and compelling argument he can present to an *outsider* is a close-up view of the transformed life of one of his *insiders*. Nothing packs a punch like a genuinely transformed life. Jesus knew that if he could get transformed believers in close relationship with seekers, good things were going to happen. What an awesome reality—Jesus' plan to reach this world is built on his work in and through our lives!

We are called to be God's agents on this earth. Before returning to heaven, Jesus told his followers that they would be his messengers, ambassadors, and witnesses. Jesus wanted all of his followers to realize that his plan to reach the world depended on them. He chooses to use individuals as spokespeople for him. He has placed the message of salvation in our hands and we have the high honor of bringing the good news to the ends of the earth.

Making the Connection

1. Describe a time when you were given a big responsibility in *one* of the following areas of life and describe how you handled that responsibility:

   ☐ In grade school

   ☐ In your family as you were growing up

   ☐ In high school or college

   ☐ In the workplace

   How do you feel when someone trusts you enough to place a significant responsibility in your hands?

Knowing and Being Known

Read Matthew 5:13 – 16

2. How does Jesus feel about salt that has lost its taste?

   What message is Jesus sending to his followers who never give witness to their faith in him?

3. Jesus says his followers are "the light of the world." What does Jesus tell his listeners to do and not to do as we live our light-filled lives?

Getting Salty

Think about salt for a moment and why Jesus chose to use salt as a metaphor for how we should go out and affect the world. What does salt do? One obvious answer is that it *makes you thirsty*. Isn't that why it is widely served in bars? They want people to eat salty pretzels, peanuts, or popcorn so they will drink more beverages.

Salt also *spices things up* a bit. Can you image corn-on-the-cob without salt? Salt enhances flavor. Many foods would be bland without a dash of salt to bring out the flavor.

Salt also *preserves*. Long before the days of the Frigidaire, salt was used to keep certain foods from spoiling. Certain meats could be preserved for long periods of time if they were packed in salt.

So salt creates thirst, enhances flavor, and preserves. This leads us to the big question: What *specifically* did Jesus have in mind when he looked at his followers and said, "You are the salt of the earth"? We don't know for certain, but maybe Jesus meant for the metaphor of salt to symbolize all three.

4. Using the following three images as a springboard, draw as many parallels as possible between salt and Christians who are seeking to make an impact for Jesus among those who are not yet his followers.

   • *Salt makes people thirsty*: How can we make people thirst for the living water of Jesus?

   • *Salt spices things up*: How can we add flavor in our community and culture?

• *Salt is a powerful preservative*: How can we be a preservative that helps to slow the erosion of the beauty and moral purity God wants to bring in this world?

5. What is one way you are actively seeking to be salt in the life of a person who is not a follower of Jesus? How can other believers pray for you in this relationship?

Letting Your Light Shine

Have you ever woken up at night and been in utter darkness? Can you remember moving slowly, cautiously, apprehensively forward as you reached out trying to find a light switch? Do you remember the blanket of darkness covering you? Do you remember when you finally found the switch, flipped it, and felt peace as the room was flooded with light?

Light illuminates dark places and helps us see where we need to go. It takes away fear and allows us to move ahead with confidence. Christians are called to be light in this world of darkness. We are to let our lives shine before the world. When the radiance of Jesus fills our lives, we naturally reflect this light to those around us. As God's light-bearers, we are called to make sure nothing keeps his light from continuing to shine in our lives.

6. List as many parallels as you can between light and Christians. Reflect on the many properties and uses for light and see how many connections you can draw.

7. Describe a life situation you are in right now where there is a great deal of darkness. How is God calling you and using you to be his light in this situation, and how can other believers support you in this ministry?

Getting Motivated

Why share our faith with others? Why was Jesus so serious about us living our lives as salt and light? Why did he give such solemn warnings for those who refuse to let their light shine and who don't live salty lives?

First of all, we share our faith because *our Savior is the absolute best!* We have a stockpile of God's blessings that have been poured into our lives. He has given us love and hope and the promise of eternity. When we live in the awareness of all God has given us, it spills over to others. We also let our light shine because we have been honored with a *heavenly invitation* to participate in this grand endeavor to bring people to faith. The God of heaven has invited all followers of Christ to share in the most important enterprise ever: to help all people become fully devoted followers of Christ. We are also moved to be more and more salty because *we know hell is real.* There are people who are headed for a Christless eternity if they don't come to know Jesus. When we look at the seekers around us, their eternal destiny should matter to us simply because it matters to God. Finally, we are committed to being his light and salt because we know that every time someone has a radical heart change and becomes a follower of Christ, *Jesus and the angels of heaven rejoice.* What a joy-filled moment when somebody says, "Thanks for leading me to Jesus . . . thanks for all of eternity!" Leading someone to the cross is the single greatest contribution you can ever make to someone's life. We need to keep these reminders firmly in our hearts and be moved to grow as salt and light.

8. Jesus clearly wants us to have high levels of motivation when it comes to being his salt and light. What is one "bowl" under which your light can sometimes get hidden?

9. What motivation have you discovered that most effectively inspires you to "put your lamp on a stand" and let your light shine?

10. Tell about a person who God used as salt and light in your life. What did that person say and do that impacted you in your faith?

How has that person's example inspired you to let your light shine and make your life more salty?

Celebrating and Being Celebrated

Lift up prayers of thanksgiving and celebration for those God has used as his salt and light in your life. Thank God for sending such wonderful people to impact you with his gospel.

Loving and Being Loved

Show your love and appreciation to one person who has had a great impact on your faith by writing a note that expresses specific ways God has used him or her to be salt and light in your life. Using some of the parallels you discussed in this study, thank this person for letting God's light shine through them. Also, encourage this person to continue having such an impact on the lives of others around him or her.

Serving and Being Served

Often the door for evangelism is opened through acts of compassionate service. Identify one person in your life who is not yet a follower of Christ, and who you feel close to. Pray about one act of caring service that God might lead you to extend to this person. As you serve this person, pray for his or her heart to grow open and soft to the love of God and the message of the gospel.

Healing Relationships

MATTHEW 5:21 – 26

THERE'S A KIND OF PROTOCOL THAT GOVERNS HOW PEOPLE BEHAVE WHEN they attend large public gatherings like concerts, movies, plays, or church services. These rules are not written down anywhere, but most of us have a sense for how these unwritten rules work.

One rule most of us agree on is that people should get to public gatherings on time. When you have taken pains to plan your time out carefully, and have arrived on time, it can be real irritating when a tardy bunch show up after the show begins. We have all had the experience of getting somewhere on time, finding our seat, and then having to deal with people who show up late and have to crawl all over us to get to their seats. Simply speaking, it's breaking the rules of etiquette.

I remember a time when I was the one breaking this rule of etiquette. I was late getting to a Chicago Bears football game. I had to crawl over a bunch of people in the middle of a seating section. Wouldn't you know it, one guy I had to get past was clearly proud of his beer belly ... and he had a lot to be proud of! It was clear that he was angry at me for being late and was not going to move for me. He just smiled at me with his belly hanging out there. I didn't know if I should climb over it or limbo under it! One thing I do know, I won't be late to another Bears game.

Another rule in large public gatherings is to be quiet. Have you ever gone to a movie or play only to sit near someone who talks or whispers throughout the whole show? When this happens, many people will give a quick glance over their shoulder and give the rude talker *the look*.

Although there are many other unwritten rules for public gatherings, there is one that seems to be at the top of the list: don't leave until the meeting is over. It is the height of rudeness to get up and climb over half a dozen people to walk out of a meeting. It's so rude, in fact, that getting up and walking out of a public setting is often recognized as a form of protest. When you see someone stand up in the middle of a large public gathering, pick up their stuff, climb over people, and leave, you think to yourself that something must be very, very wrong. This is true in our day, and it was true in Jesus' day as well. As a matter of fact, in those days, walking out of a church service would have been unthinkable!

Making the Connection

1. What are some of the rules of etiquette in our society?

Tell about a time when you, or someone else you know, broke a rule of etiquette.

Knowing and Being Known

Read Matthew 5:21 – 22

2. Jesus quotes from the Ten Commandments (Exodus 20:13 and Deuteronomy 5:17) and reminds the people that murder is a sin. Then Jesus raises the righteousness bar by giving three examples of other behaviors about which God is deeply concerned. What are these three behaviors, and what consequences might we face if we engage in them?

Behavior		Possible Consequence
_____	can lead to	_____
_____	can lead to	_____
_____	can lead to	_____

3. What is Jesus teaching us about *one* of the areas of life listed below?

☐ When we carry unresolved and growing anger in our heart toward another person

☐ When our anger toward someone leads us to begin to see them, treat them, or call them a fool

☐ When we get in the habit of name-calling or using words that have the spirit of a word like *raca* (the NIV Study Bible states, "*Raca* may be related to the Aramaic word for 'empty' and mean 'empty-headed'")

4. What is a time or situation when you are most tempted to lose your temper and let your words get out of control? What does this teaching of Jesus have to say to you in this area of your life?

A Huge Breach of Etiquette

First-century church services were often modeled after synagogue gatherings. When you attended religious services in the first century, you showed up on time. You didn't even think about walking into a synagogue late. You didn't poke your neighbor, tell jokes during the service, text or answer your cell phone . . . no, no, no! You can bet your life you didn't get up in front of everybody halfway through the sermon and climb over six people to leave. If you suddenly remembered the pot roast was set too high back home, you just considered it a burnt offering unto the Lord. If you were feeling deathly ill, you took comfort in knowing that your passing would be duly acknowledged by the church leaders *after* the service.

Against this background Jesus says something unthinkable. He issues free passes for people to get up in the middle of any church service and leave . . . even during the sermon. He gives them permission to stand up, gather their stuff, climb over sixteen people, and head for the exits, provided they are leaving for the *right reason*. What is this right reason? Jesus says that the only justifiable cause for walking out in the middle of a worship service is if you are going to repair a broken relationship. If you realize you have a strained or damaged relationship, God gives permission for you to leave so you can attempt to reconcile with this person.

5. Read Matthew 5:23–24 slowly and carefully. Then, use the space provided below to put this passage in your own words for our day and age.

Why do you feel Jesus is telling people to do something so dramatic?

6. Jesus seems to be making a connection between our relationship with others and our relationship with God. How does having strong and healthy relationships with others impact your spiritual life and growth?

How does living with broken and conflict-filled relationships affect you as a worshiper and follower of Christ?

7. Describe a broken relationship you are dealing with right now. (If you are using this study in a small group and the relationship is with a person that your group members may know, do not use a name or give telling information.) Then pray (or ask for prayer) as you seek reconciliation in this relationship.

Rules for Reconciliation

I wish I could provide an easy formula for healing broken relationships, but relationships aren't that simple. Every relationship is unique. However, there are some very important biblical guidelines that can help as you seek restoration in broken relationships.

First, when you walk in the room, how you carry yourself, *your demeanor*, will make a big difference in the reconciliation attempt. If you come into the room with the spirit of power, intimidation, self-righteousness, or arrogance, the other person can smell it a mile away. If you come with a humble spirit and a gentle heart, you will be well on your way to healing.

Second, when it comes time to talk, make a *clear statement of your intentions*. Say something like, "Bob, I think we both know things have gone south between us. But, you know, I really didn't come here to go toe-to-toe on everything we disagree about. What I really want to say is that I would like to reestablish our relationship, even if we can't agree on lots of stuff. I pray that we can find healing in our relationship." Be absolutely clear about where you want to go with this relationship.

Third, be ready to *extend forgiveness and to be forgiven*. This means you do not stand there and tap your foot until the other person apologizes. Be ready to own your part of the breakdown very early in the talk and humbly ask to be forgiven. Extend forgiveness to the other person and do not hold their sins against them.

Read Matthew 5:25 – 26

8. What illustration does Jesus use to help us see the importance of seeking healing in broken relationships, and why do you think Jesus has such a sense of urgency?

9. Make a list of some of the things in a person's demeanor that will help or hinder a reconciliation attempt:

What will be helpful?   **What will not help?**

10. In what one area from the previous list do you need to work on having a positive demeanor in your next effort at relational reconciliation?

How can your Christian friends pray for you and encourage you as you grow in this area?

Celebrating and Being Celebrated

Jesus calls us to go out of our way to seek relational reconciliation and healing. Not only does he call us to do this, but he gives us a perfect example of what it looks like. Jesus left the glory of heaven and gave his own life so that we could be brought back into relationship with God. Lift up prayers of thankfulness for all that Jesus has done to bring you back into a restored relationship with the Father.

Loving and Being Loved

Jesus teaches us that our words have tremendous power. He gives very specific warning about the damage we can do (to others and ourselves) when we use harsh terms like "dummy," "stupid," "idiot," "airhead," and other such names. Take time in the coming week to do a vocabulary assessment. Think through the terms you use to describe others when you are angry or frustrated. Reflect on what you say in the workplace. Inventory the things you say when you are with your friends. Think about what your children hear you say when you are driving in the car and someone cuts you off. Be honest about any negative terms that might have slipped into your vocabulary.

Follow the teaching of Jesus and grow in your love for others as you commit to removing these harsh terms from your vocabulary. You might even want to let a couple of close friends or family members know that you have decided that certain terms are now off limits for you. Tell them that if you use any of these terms to describe another person, you want a reminder that you are seeking to show love to others by *not* using such pain-filled names.

Serving and Being Served

We all have people in our lives who have modeled a great example of what it means to be a mature follower of Jesus Christ. Identify a person who has been an example of maturity in relationships for you. During the coming week, bless that person by letting him or her know how God has used them in your life as an example and encouragement in your relationships.

Looking, Lusting, or Loving?

MATTHEW 5:27 – 30

HAVE YOU EVER BEEN STRUCK BY THE POWER OF THE HUMAN IMAGINATION? Our imaginations can transport us to another place in an instant. Try it for a moment. Close your eyes and transport yourself mentally to your favorite vacation place. Where are you? Are you in the majesty and grandeur of the mountains? The dry heat of the desert? Along the ocean or one of the Great Lakes? You might be in the city or at a favorite cottage away from the hustle and busyness of the world, or maybe you're in another country.

Now allow yourself to picture the home where you spent most of your time growing up. Can you see the dinner table where you spent most of your meals as a family? Do you remember where everyone sat? You can probably remember what you had for dinner on certain nights of the week. If you linger there long enough in your imagination, you might even begin to hear the sounds and even smell the smells of your old kitchen.

This thing called the imagination is really something. Using it, we can go places without moving a muscle. We can replay pleasant memories of the past without pushing a rewind button and can project ourselves into future scenarios. It helps us maintain a spirit of courage during times of difficulty, because we can imagine what life will be like when we get through it. Imagination also stimulates creativity. It helps leaders develop a vision for the future of their organization. Imagination is a marvelous gift from the hand of a creative God.

Making the Connection

1. God has given us powerful imaginations. When you close your eyes and imagine being in your favorite vacation place, what do you see, hear, smell, taste, and feel?

When you think back to the family dinner table in the home where you grew up, what do you see, hear, smell, taste, and feel?

Knowing and Being Known

The Shadow Side of Our Imagination

Although imagination is, without a doubt, a wonderful gift from God, there is also a shadow side to our ability to imagine. This shadow side is our ability to imagine ourselves in dishonoring, self-destructive scenarios. Because nobody around us has any idea what's going on inside our minds and hearts, we can enter this dark inner world and still look good on the outside. As you know by now, Jesus' teaching in the Sermon on the Mount is calling us to go way beyond surface Christianity and to look deeply at what lies in our hearts.

I remember talking to a guy who told me that he hated his job. More specifically, he hated his boss. He told me he was having a recurring fantasy in which he mustered up the courage to walk into his boss's office, picked him up by the lapels, screamed obscenities at him, hung him on the chandelier above the desk, and walked out. I said, "Do you really think about that kind of stuff?" He said, "I've done it in my head a hundred times. It makes me feel good. I can get even with my boss without losing my job. It's only a mind game, and nobody knows about it."

Our imagination allows us to play a negative mental tape over and over again. We can lash out in anger and hurt another person without lifting a finger. We can place ourselves in lust-producing mental situations and still appear pure on the outside. Jesus wants us to beware of the shadow side of our imagination.

Read Matthew 5:27 – 30

2. Jesus is quoting from Exodus 20:14 and Deuteronomy 5:18. Look at the context of this quote in both of these passages and discuss why these words of Jesus would have been so significant to his hearers.

3. Jesus tells his hearers that it is time to raise the righteousness bar a notch and move beyond the letter of the Law to the spirit of the Law. How does this teaching of Jesus challenge all of us to examine our hearts?

4. In light of what Jesus teaches in this passage, what do you think he would say in response to *one* of the following statements?

   ☐ At a bachelor party, a friend of the groom leans over and whispers to the groom, "In two days you will be married. You can't touch other women, but that doesn't mean you can't keep looking!"

   ☐ A woman is talking to a friend about a coworker. She says, "I have lusted after that man a hundred times. I might as well go ahead and have an affair with him. The Bible says I have done it in my heart already ... so what's the difference?"

   ☐ A TV ad agent says to a marketing team, "Let's show as much skin as we can in this commercial. We all know that sex sells! It won't hurt anyone and it will boost our sales!"

☐ A high school student says to his friend, "I'm a Christian, and my girlfriend and I are committed to wait until we are married to have sex. When I feel tempted, I just leave her, spend some time looking at women in magazines and on the Internet, and then I feel satisfied. I think God understands that this is what I need to do so I can honor him in my dating relationship."

God's Ideal

The Bible says that both men and women are created in the image of God. There is a part of us that reflects his character, his identity, and his personality. This means God wants us to relate to each other in a way that reflects the health and holiness that he can bring to our relationships. When a man looks upon a woman, and when a woman looks upon a man, God wants us to see a person! In other words, when a man looks at a woman he needs to be aware of all she is, and not simply be fixated on her physical appearance. He needs to realize that this image-bearing person has an intellectual side and say to himself, *I wonder what this woman thinks about.* He should realize she has an emotional side and think, *I wonder what this woman is feeling these days, how her emotional patterns work. What are her highs and lows? What is she happy about and what is she sad about?* He should acknowledge her relational side and ask himself, *I wonder what kind of family this woman came from and what her friendships are like.* He should see a spiritual dimension and think, *I wonder what she believes about God. I wonder whether she has faith. I wonder what her spiritual beliefs are like.* God's ideal is that we would see each other as multidimensional image-bearing people and not just physical bodies to be admired!

Read Genesis 1:26 – 28; 2:20 – 25

5. As you read these passages from Genesis, what do you learn?

• About how God made us

• About who we are in relationship to God and each other

• About how much God values us

6. How does God feel about human sexuality when it is expressed within the boundaries he has established?

How do you think God wants us to view human sexuality?

Life in the Real World

We live in a sin-stained world where we are bombarded with sexual images, tantalizing pictures, seductive models, revealing magazines, movies with sexual themes, TV shows that keep expanding the boundaries of what is considered appropriate for prime-time or daytime shows, and countless other images that can draw us into a lustful condition of heart. There is no escaping it! This constant assault can produce sexual energy in us that threatens to come out in some pretty ill-defined and unpredictable ways. We don't live in a cocoon that separates us from these messages, so we need to acknowledge the battle and be ready to fight!

Read Matthew 5:29 – 30

7. What dramatic images does Jesus use to help us understand the seriousness of lusting?

If Jesus is not calling us to literally mutilate ourselves (and he is not), then what *is* he teaching us?

8. What are some of the sources of lust-producing thoughts we face in our culture?

9. What are some practical ways we can begin to "cut off" the source of these lust-producing images and situations?

A Sober Warning

Jesus knows that we have powerful imaginations that can be used for good and for evil. He also warns us that on the shadow side of our imaginations is a very dark place where some people begin to live. Many church-going people loved by God — followers of Christ who look great on the outside — are living with serious sexual addictions and obsessions. One gentleman wrote me a letter about the pain of his own struggle in this area of his life:

"Dear Bill, I'm an emotional invalid. Lust is eating me up. It perverts my view of women. It distorts my social life. It wreaks havoc in my emotional stability. It paralyzes my spiritual life and destroys any possibility of God using me in this church. Recently, I've become addicted to pornography, which has intensified the problem. The sad part is that I know that lust and pornography promise everything and produce nothing, but I still just can't seem to stop."

10. In the letter above the man struggling with sexual obsession writes, "Lust and pornography promise everything and produce nothing." What do you think he means?

11. What counsel would you give to a follower of Christ who has become caught in the web of intense lusting and pornography?

Celebrating and Being Celebrated

As you close this study, pray in three specific directions:

1. Lift up prayers thanking God for the wonder that he made us male and female. Celebrate God's good plan of human sexuality.
2. Pray for strength to keep your mind, heart, and life pure in the way you relate to others.
3. Pray for those who feel trapped and unable to get out of unhealthy patterns of thinking and acting when it comes to their own sexuality. Lift up prayers of praise that God's power is great enough to overcome even these kinds of struggles!

Loving and Being Loved

Take time in the coming weeks to memorize Matthew 5:27–30 and 1 Timothy 5:1–2. Pray for God to give you a pure heart and a loving spirit toward others. If you have developed unhealthy behaviors or thought patterns, pray for God to use his Word to cleanse and transform your heart.

Serving and Being Served

If you are a parent, your patterns and lifestyle will impact your children. Inventory the images you are inviting into your mind and home. Evaluate the television channels you subscribe to. What magazines do you keep around the house? What websites do you surf? Are there patterns in your life that would damage your son or daughter if those patterns were passed on to the next generation? Serve your family by cutting off any source of lust-producing images in your home.

Truth-Telling

MATTHEW 5:33 – 37

SOME YEARS AGO A DEAR FRIEND OF MINE, LEE STROBEL, PREACHED ON THE topic of truth-telling. He gave an illustration that I wish to retell as we begin thinking about the call of Jesus to be people who speak the truth.

Nearly three hundred years ago in England, there lived a great commander of a merchant ship. His name was Captain Fudge. Yes, this was an actual historical figure! With time, Captain Fudge became notorious for telling all kinds of lies, tall tales, and exaggerations about his improbable adventures on the high seas.

In fact, Captain Fudge's name became so identified with stretching the truth that whenever his crew would hear somebody else tell a tall tale, they would point a finger and say, "Fudge, Fudge." After a while his fame even spread to America. By the mid-1800s when kids would try to cheat at marbles, their opponents would yell, "No fudging!"

To this day, the term "fudging" is used when someone is lying, cheating, hedging, or misrepresenting something. We might say, "Oh, he fudges on his income tax," or "That candidate made a lot of promises, but now look what's happened ... he's starting to fudge."

Let's face it, at one time or another everyone is tempted to fudge a little. None of us is totally honest all of the time. We occasionally exaggerate. We tend to break our commitments from time to time. In fact, we can trace this kind of misbehavior all the way back to the opening scenes of the Bible, when Adam fudged by blaming Eve for the way they had violated God's command. Another example is when Cain killed his brother and then fudged when God asked him about it. Ever since the earliest days of human history, the world has feasted on fudge. Sadly, we still do!

THE PERSPECTIVES OF JESUS

Making the Connection

1. What are some ways people still fudge today?

   • In the workplace

   • In their relationships

   • In their personal goals and commitments

Knowing and Being Known

Read Matthew 5:33 – 37

2. What were some of the things people used to swear by in Jesus' day, and why do you think they did this?

3. What kind of oaths do people make today—in other words, what sort of things do they say to try to convince people they are telling the truth?

What advice does Jesus have for people who feel the need to make oaths and swear so that others will believe them?

4. Jesus says that anything beyond a yes or a no comes from the evil one. What do you think Jesus is trying to teach us with these strong words?

A Handshake Used to Be Enough!

There was a day when a handshake was enough to seal a deal. Two people looked at each other, made an agreement, and shook hands. Their word was their bond. Today, virtually no one does business without a written contract and a team of lawyers at their side. Rather than trust, there is suspicion. Rather than an expectation that all parties will keep their word and uphold their side of the agreement, every precaution is taken to be sure no one gets burned. Still, despite all the paperwork and contractual safety nets in place, there seem to be more and more broken promises and agreements than ever.

5. In Jesus' day, an oath was taken very seriously. Promises, commitments, and oaths seem to be viewed differently today. How would you define the modern-day view of commitments and promises in *one* of the following areas?

☐ In business agreements

☐ In a marriage covenant

☐ In a court of law

☐ In any area we make promises

6. Although some people treat broken promises and commitments as a small, insignificant matter, what results can come when a person regularly fails to keep his or her word?

7. Jesus said, "Let your 'Yes' be 'Yes,' and your 'No' be 'No.'" He calls us to honesty and integrity in our words. Who is one person you know who lives a life with this kind of habitual honesty? How has his or her example and lifestyle influenced your life?

It Starts with the Little Things

God is concerned that we become habitual truth-tellers. He knows that we won't be ready to tell the truth in the big areas of life if we can't even tell the truth in the little things. Read the list below and think about how easy it is to make statements that are simply not true.

1. The doctor will be with you shortly.
2. We'll get together for lunch sometime soon.
3. Just give me a call if you have a need . . . I'll be there for you.
4. I'll pay you back tomorrow.
5. I'll respect you in the morning.
6. I'll just take a minute of your time.
7. As long as we both shall live.
8. This is going to hurt me more than it will hurt you.
9. The check is in the mail.
10. I'll be praying for you.

If we are going to honor God by being truth-tellers in the big areas of life, we need to learn to measure our words and be sure we are speaking the truth in every situation.

8. Look at the previous list and think about how easy it is to "bend the truth," tell "little white lies," and "break promises." What is one area that comes to mind in which you need to grow in your commitment to let your yes be yes and your no be no?

9. What are some practical steps you can take to become a consistent truth-teller?

10. If you have broken a promise or a commitment you have made to another person, what steps can you take to restore that relationship and seek a new beginning?

Celebrating and Being Celebrated

Our God is a promise-keeping God. He never lies! Reflect on any of the promises God has given in his Word. Celebrate the reality that you can live with rock-solid confidence that he will always keep his promises. As you pray, consider praying some of these words of Scripture back to God and thank him for making such amazing promises.

Loving and Being Loved

During the coming week, ask God to speak to you about any areas in which you have been breaking commitments. Use one of the following prayers to get you started:

- Lord of love, are there people I have been hurting and disappointing because I have been consistently breaking my word?
- God of truth, are there areas of my life in which I have begun to tell lies and bend the truth to suit my own desires? Please show me if this has been happening. Make me humble to hear your voice and be willing to change!

If God puts a person on your heart and convicts you of the need to ask for his or her forgiveness, do this as soon as possible. It might be a spouse, a child or parent, a friend or coworker. Whoever it is, go to that person with a broken heart and ask for his or her forgiveness for the ways you have betrayed trust through breaking your commitments. Let him or her know that you want a restored relationship and that you will be seeking God's strength to become a person who keeps their word in every situation.

Serving and Being Served

The challenge that follows is not a 101-level challenge. This is a 401 class in serving, so take this on only if you feel called by God. Consider serving a close friend by being a truth-teller with him or her. If you have a close friend who has made a habit of breaking promises in his relationship with you, consider sitting down with him and sharing what you have learned in this study. Let him know that you love him, but that you have been hurt by the way he has broken promises and commitments he has made to you. Let him know that God offers power for him to become a person whose yes means yes and whose no means no.

THE
PRAYER
of JESUS

John Ortberg

The "Who," "Where," and "What" of Prayer

MATTHEW 6:5 – 15

HAS YOUR MIND EVER WANDERED WHILE YOU WERE PRAYING? YOU WANT TO be focused and engaged in the experience, but the next thing you know you are wondering if you remembered to turn off the stove, if you closed the garage door, or if you should take a vacation next summer. A wandering mind is something we all face as we seek to become people of prayer.

Psychologists talk about a condition they call "mindlessness." For some of us, mindlessness is a problem we suffer occasionally in prayer and in life. For others, mindlessness *is* a way of life. We can be physically present, but our minds are floating off somewhere in space, on autopilot.

Jesus taught that mindlessness is one of the biggest obstacles to prayer. He said, "And when you pray, do not keep on babbling like pagans, for they think they will be heard because of their many words" (Matthew 6:7). Jesus knew that prayer can sometimes deteriorate into mindless babble or "sacred" worrying. We all have experienced this. We begin praying sincerely only to start rambling through a series of words with no idea of what we're saying.

Jesus gave the prayer recorded in Matthew 6:9–13 as a tool to help us get beyond such mindlessness. He intended to give us a simple structure and some helpful themes and categories to focus on so that we could remain mindful as we pray. Sadly, in many church traditions we have made the recitation of this prayer a mindless routine. Week after week we repeat the words, but our minds and hearts are not engaged. Jesus was looking for exactly the opposite. He wanted this prayer to become a springboard into the deep, refreshing waters of intimate conversation with the God we love. Indeed, Christians have used it this way for over two thousand years.

When we pray "Our Father," we should be moved to reflect deeply on the person and tender care of God. When we say, "Hallowed be your name," we should be inspired to give him worship, adoration, and praise. If we dare to declare, "Your will be done," we should be propelled into prayers of submission and surrender. As we ask for our "daily bread," we should find ourselves humbly telling God about the needs we have in our lives and in the lives of those we love. Jesus did not give us a prayer to memorize and repeat over and over until our minds go blank. It is a launchpad from which we are lifted to high places of worship, petition, confession, and so much more. Every time we pray this prayer, something new and fresh can happen.

Making the Connection

1. If you grew up reciting the Lord's Prayer in church or your home, how was this prayer used?

If you did not grow up with this prayer, what is your perception of how it is understood and used by Christians?

Knowing and Being Known

Read Matthew 6:5 – 15

2. As you read Matthew 6:9 – 13, what are the "big themes" that Jesus is teaching us to focus on as we pray?

   •

   •

-

-

-

-

-

Which of these themes do you find most natural to pray about? How do you enter into prayer about this topic or theme?

3. Which theme in the Lord's Prayer tends to get neglected as you engage in conversations with God?

How do you hope this study will help you go deeper in this area of your prayer life?

The "Who" of Prayer

Have you ever felt guilty about your prayer life? Most of us have. The reason for this low-grade guilt is what I call a "who" problem. We get confused about the nature of the person to whom we are praying. We start to think that God is angry with us or at least a little disappointed. This "who" problem can keep us from growing more passionate, intimate, and effective in prayer.

Jesus begins this prayer with the words, "Our Father." When we begin praying, it is important to stop our hurried minds and acknowledge the fact that we are speaking to *someone*. God is personal. When Jesus taught his followers to say "Our Father," he introduced the most unique opening line in the history of prayer.

Every time we use a name, we make a statement about the nature of the relationship. That's why names are so powerful. In formal relationships we might say "Mr." or "Mrs." If we are talking to a friend, we usually call them by their first name. If it's a real close friend, sometimes we use a nickname. When we say "Father" or "Daddy," we are expressing that we are in an intimate family relationship.

Read Romans 8:15 – 17 and Galatians 4:6 – 7

4. When Jesus invited us to address God as "Father," he understood that none of us has perfect earthly fathers. If we think of our heavenly Father as being a cosmic version of our earthly father, we will have a confused prayer life (no matter how good or bad our earthly father has been). Instead, Jesus is teaching us that we have a perfect, loving, and powerful Father in heaven. What kinds of things would a great earthly father do for his children?

What sorts of things does our Father in heaven want to do for his children?

5. Some people don't like the idea of addressing God as "Father." What might we lose if we do away with calling God our Father?

6. How have you experienced God's fatherly love, protection, or provision?

The "Where" of Prayer

Jesus teaches us to pray to "Our Father in heaven." How far away is heaven? We tend to think of heaven as someplace in outer space. As a result, we can imagine that God is remote, distant, and hard to access.

To correct this misconception it helps to know a little background on the grammar of the phrase "Our Father in heaven." The Greek word for heaven is *uranos*, from which we get the word for our planet Uranus. In the Lord's Prayer, it is the plural form of the word. Literally the prayer is, "Our Father, the one in the heavens." This phrase is used a variety of ways in the New Testament: for the atmosphere, for the sky, and also for the air we breathe.

It is this final sense of the word that Jesus intends in this prayer. When you pray, "Our Father who is in the heavens," you are saying, "Our Father who is all around me," "Our Father who is closer than the air I breathe," "Our Father who is right here, right now." God is that close! We are never alone.

7. What makes us feel that God is far away and that there is a great distance between us and him?

8. How have you experienced God's nearness and presence in your life?

9. If God were sitting in a chair right in front of you, what would you ask him? What would you tell him?

How might your prayer life change if you knew God was sitting beside you, ready to hear what is on your heart?

The "What" of Prayer

Most of us have times when we are not exactly sure what we ought to pray about. This "what" problem can get in our way. We're not sure what God might be interested in. Does he really care about the little stuff of life? Is he all that interested in the things that matter to me? The truth is that there is no concern, no matter how small, that God does not care about. There is no request, no matter how silly or trivial it may seem, that God doesn't want to hear. He wants us to talk with him about everything, even our daily bread. God cares about the little things and the big things of life.

However, at this point I want to note the very first request included in the Lord's Prayer is, "Hallowed be your name." A name in the Bible is never just a label. It's a reflection of the person, his or her character and identity. We are to "hallow" or give the honor that is due to the name of God. To God himself! We are to praise, revere, and exalt the name of God.

Read Exodus 20:7 and Psalm 66:1 – 4

10. Why do you think God is so concerned that his name not be misused?

What are some of the ways the name of God is abused and misused, and how can we seek to honor his name in a world that tends to trample on it?

11. Throughout the Bible there are many names for God. What is a name for God that you love, and what does this name express about God's character and nature?

Celebrating and Being Celebrated

Use the Lord's Prayer to guide your prayer time. Offer up brief prayers that grow naturally out of each portion of the prayer:

- Our Father in heaven, hallowed be your name,
- Your kingdom come, your will be done on earth as it is in heaven.
- Give us today our daily bread.
- Forgive us our debts, as we also have forgiven our debtors.
- Lead us not into temptation, but deliver us from the evil one.

Loving and Being Loved

In our human relationships we express love through our bodies. We give hugs and kisses. We smile. We give a wink or a nod to say "I love you and you matter to me." In a very similar way we can express love to God through our body language. In particular, our posture in prayer can be a way to communicate love to the God who loves us without reservation.

What posture do you use when you pray? What do you do with your eyes? What do you do with your body? How do you use your hands?

Some people have grown up in a tradition where they heard, "Every head bowed, every eye closed," when it was time to pray. This might feel like a hard and fast biblical rule, but the truth is, the Bible never tells us to close our eyes and fold our hands. These are things we teach children so they won't get distracted or poke other kids during prayer time.

According to the Bible, Jesus' common posture for prayer was "he stood and looked into the heavens." Scripture also records, among other stances, people praying as they knelt, as they lay prostrate on the ground, as they sat with their hands stretched out, and with faces lifted toward the sky or bowed down toward the earth. The point is that there is not an exact posture of prayer, but we should engage our bodies in our expression of prayer.

Experiment this week with different physical expressions as you pray. Find something that feels right as you do your best to express love to the God who calls you his child.

Serving and Being Served

If you have children, grandchildren, nieces, nephews, or young people you can influence, consider teaching them to pray the Lord's Prayer. Don't just help them memorize the words and repeat them over and over. Teach them to use this great prayer as a springboard into deep and refreshing places of conversation with God.

Your Kingdom Come

MATTHEW 6:10

KEN DAVIS RECOUNTS A STORY FROM THE DAYS WHEN MIKE DITKA WAS COACH-ing the Chicago Bears football team. Davis writes:

> One day Ditka was about to deliver a locker room pep talk and he looked up and saw defensive tackle William "Refrigerator" Perry. Then again, how could he NOT see him? At 338 pounds the Fridge stood out even in a crowd of pro football players! Ditka gestured to the Fridge and said, "When I get finished I'd like you to close with the Lord's Prayer." Then the coach began his talk.
>
> Meanwhile, Jim McMahon, the brash and outspoken quarterback, punched John Cassis and whispered, "Look at Perry, he doesn't know the Lord's Prayer." Sure enough Perry sat with a look of panic on his face, his head in his hands, sweating profusely. Cassis replied, "Nah ... sure he does! He's just nervous. Everybody knows the Lord's Prayer!" After a few minutes of watching the Refrigerator leak several gallons of sweat, McMahon nudged Cassis again and said, "I'll bet you fifty bucks Fridge doesn't know the Lord's Prayer."
>
> When Coach Ditka finished his pep talk, he asked all the men to remove their caps. Then he nodded at Perry and bowed his head. The room was quiet for a few moments before the Fridge began to speak in a shaky voice and said, "Now I lay me down to sleep. I pray the Lord, my soul to keep ..."
>
> Cassis felt a tap on his shoulder. It was Jim McMahon who whispered to him, "You win. Here's the fifty dollars. I had no idea Perry knew the Lord's Prayer."

People are not born knowing the Lord's Prayer. And those who learn it often fail to really understand the depth and significance of what they are praying. One line of the prayer that seems to be the least understood of all is, "Your kingdom come, your will be done, on earth as it is in heaven" (Matthew 6:10). Most Christians do not have a great deal of clarity on what the kingdom of heaven is. There's a good reason for this. We can barely understand what this earth would look like if God's kingdom were to really break into human history. It boggles the mind.

One technical phrase that's often used to define the kingdom of God is the "range of God's effective will." Imagine everything that God desires to happen actually happening—the time, place, and reality when all he desires is what we experience. That's God's kingdom.

Making the Connection

1. If God's kingdom were to break fully into human history while you sleep tonight, what is one thing that would be different when you wake up tomorrow morning?

Knowing and Being Known

Read Matthew 6:9 – 15

2. What is something you know God desires for this world in *one* of the following areas?

☐ In marriages   ☐ In your nation

☐ In families   ☐ In the life of the local church

3. Followers of Christ are called to pray for God's will to be done. We are also expected to do our part to help bring about kingdom transformation in our world. Considering the items listed in question two, what is one action you could take to be part of God's plan to bring his kingdom to this earth?

4. As you think about the life and ministry of Jesus, what were some of the signs that the kingdom of God was breaking into human history?

The Kingdom Is Near ... The Kingdom Is Here

Jesus lifted up the message of God's kingdom over and over. It was the core of his gospel. In Mark we read, "After John was put in prison, Jesus went into Galilee, proclaiming the good news of God. 'The time has come,' he said. 'The kingdom of God has come near. Repent and believe the good news!'" (Mark 1:14 – 15). When Jesus says the kingdom of God is near, he's not saying it's getting kind of close. He's saying that it's available now. It has broken into human history; it's here!

In human history, there is only one life that has been lived in which God's will had total unhindered sway. Jesus bore in his own person, in his flesh and blood, the reality of the kingdom of God. Everybody who saw him saw a life lived in the reality of God, a life in which whatever God desired became reality. But the story does not end there. Jesus lets his followers know that it is now possible for human beings to live in the presence and power of God. We can do it right now. The kingdom is near ... the kingdom is here. We can live a life saturated with the presence and power of God, we really can.

5. Though there is turmoil and trouble in the world today, God is still on the move and his kingdom is near and here. As you look at your life, your church, other followers of Jesus you know, and the work of God around the world, what are some of the signs you see that assure you that God's kingdom is near and here?

Kingdoms in Conflict

It would be glorious if only one kingdom were at work in this world. But that is simply not the case. There was Caesar's kingdom in Jesus' day, and there are many political and economic kingdoms today, all exercising power and flexing their muscles, seeking to have influence over us. Besides these, there are entertainment kingdoms, athletic kingdoms, educational kingdoms, and the list goes on. And, of course, spiritual forces also are at work in the heavenly realms, trying to keep us from walking in the power of God's kingdom. If we are going to be successful in praying for God's kingdom to come and walking in the power of his kingdom, we must be ready to resist the lures of other false kingdoms.

God's kingdom is near and here, but one day it will come in all its fullness. One day there will be no other kingdoms. There will come a time when every other kingdom will be swept away and we will experience God's rule and authority unleashed in all its glory. What a day that will be!

Read Daniel 2:29 – 45

6. This passage in Daniel is one of many in the Bible that bring the same powerful and hope-filled message about God and his kingdom. How does this particular passage bring hope for those of us who are praying for God's kingdom to come and his will to be done?

7. How do you see the kingdoms of this world at war with the values and vision of God's kingdom?

How can we resist and fight against the influence of the world's kingdoms as we pray for God's kingdom to come?

Becoming Kingdom Pray-ers

How will God's kingdom come to earth? Amazingly, it all starts with prayer. This is why Jesus calls us to cry out, "Your kingdom come." Jesus asks you and me to be kingdom pray-ers. We do this as we pray in three distinct directions.

First, pray that the kingdom of God will break into your life and invade your soul. Pray that God would have full rule in every area of your life; hold nothing back. This could become the most powerful, dangerous, and transformational prayer you ever lift up. Next, pray for God's kingdom power and presence to be unleashed in the church and among other believers. It must begin among God's people, his followers. Then, pray for an in-breaking of the kingdom of God in our world. Pray that false kingdoms will fall and that the rule of God will sweep through political structures, economic systems, and all other human kingdoms.

Read 2 Corinthians 10:3 – 6 and Ephesians 6:10 – 18

8. What are some specific ways you can pray for each of the following?

• For the kingdom of God to break into your life on every level

- For God's kingdom to be unleashed and realized in power in the life of the local church

- For the kingdom to come in culture and society

9. Every society has kingdoms and spiritual strongholds that resist the kingdom of God. What are some of the little or big kingdoms in your community and society that God wants you to pray against?

What actions might you add to your prayers in an effort to see these kingdoms fall and the kingdom of God come?

Becoming Kingdom Bearers

When we dare to boldly pray, "Your kingdom come, your will be done," we are declaring to heaven and earth, "I'm ready to suffer for the cause of Jesus. I'm ready to endure whatever it takes to help usher in God's kingdom. I am ready to take up the cross and enter the spiritual battle that is already raging." This prayer goes beyond just the battle, but it is certainly part of what we are expressing.

We are also declaring, "God, may I become the kind of person who does your will from my heart. May your kingdom come to earth in my life. May I be a kingdom bearer." When we become kingdom pray-ers, the next logical step is that we are transformed into kingdom bearers. We begin to dream about and experience what it looks like when the kingdom of God begins to break into our lives — into our workplaces, families, relationships, financial choices, motives, and even our dreams. When we become kingdom bearers, everything changes.

Read Matthew 16:24 – 26

10. What are some of the consequences and costs you might face if you become a consistent kingdom pray-er and bearer?

11. What is one way you can be a kingdom bearer in a specific area of your life in the coming week?

How can your Christian friends pray for you and cheer you on as you seek to bear the kingdom of God in this area of your life?

Celebrating and Being Celebrated

We have the amazing privilege of being kingdom pray-ers. In question eight you noted some specific ways you can pray for God's kingdom to come. Use those reflections to lead you in a time of prayer for the in-breaking of the kingdom of God in your life, in your church, and in our world.

Loving and Being Loved

One important aspect of bearing the kingdom of God into the world is reaching out to people who are far from God. Identify at least one person God has placed in your life who is spiritually disconnected. Commit to pray for God's kingdom to invade and break into his or her life. Also, pray for opportunities to bear the presence and power of Jesus in your life as you interact with this person.

Serving and Being Served

Get a map of your area and begin praying for God's kingdom to come and his will to be done in each town. Pray for cities, communities, and neighborhoods by name. You might want to post this map where you will see it on a regular basis and use it as a prayer prompter.

Daily Bread

MATTHEW 6:11

JESUS TAUGHT US TO PRAY, "GIVE US TODAY OUR DAILY BREAD."

You can picture it, and so can I. A sixteen-year-old girl stands at her open closet door packed from floor to ceiling with shirts, pants, dresses, shoes, sweaters, coats, and all kinds of other clothes. Her eyes scan back and forth, up and down. She pushes clothes on hangers left and right, looking for something ... anything that suits her fancy. Her face is locked in an expression bordering somewhere between disappointment and disgust. Then she says it. While standing in front of a wall of clothes that could dress a medium-sized village of people, she cries out, "I don't have anything to wear!"

Jesus taught us to pray, "Give us today our daily bread."

A thirteen-year-old boy spends five minutes rummaging through the kitchen cupboards and refrigerator looking for a snack. He scans the six kinds of cereal lined up in colorful boxes. He passes over two kinds of toaster pastries because the fruity filling (with little actual fruit) is not his favorite. He snarls in disgust at the half-dozen beverage options because someone else has finished his favorite flavor of soda and has dared to leave the empty bottle in the fridge just to taunt him. At last he shouts at the top of his lungs, so his parents, the neighbors, and all of heaven can hear, "There's nothing to eat in this house!"

Jesus taught us to pray, "Give us today our daily bread."

It is painful to watch a teenager complain about "nothing to wear" or "nothing to eat," when most of them actually have more than enough. Sadly, this attitude does not seem to go away as we grow past adolescence into adulthood. In some cases, it only gets worse. We can find ourselves comparing what we have to those around us, only adding to the feeling that we don't have enough.

How do we learn to pray for daily bread when eight-year-olds carry around cell phones that cost as much as a family's full-year income in many parts of the world? What does it mean to ask God for enough bread for the day when we live in a meat-and-potato world? What does this portion of the Lord's Prayer say to those living in a time of abundance and plenty?

Making the Connection

1. Give an example of a person (yourself or someone else) who expressed the feeling that they did not have enough, but in reality, they had so much.

How do you think God feels when his children stand at a full closet or refrigerator and complain that they need more?

Knowing and Being Known

Read Matthew 6:11

The Power of Perspective

One of the best ways to understand what it means to pray for, and live with, daily bread is to relate closely with people who really do need a loaf of bread (or pot of beans or pan of rice) for the new day. If they don't have it, they will be in desperate straits.

Many churches have made a commitment to take adults and students on mission trips or plunge experiences. These "perspective-giving" adventures allow people to come face to face with poverty and pain they might not see in their normal day. After returning from a mission trip to the Dominican Republic or a remote place in Africa, people are changed. After serving a Thanksgiving meal to people who are living on the streets, they gain new perspective. These poignant moments are transformational and radically affect our attitudes and lifestyles ... for a week or two!

Sadly, a brief foray into the inner city or another country often impacts us for only a short time. Then we resume life as usual. What we need to learn is how to daily adjust our perspective so we are consistently aware of how much we really do have.

2. Describe a moment when you experienced a perspective shift and realized how much you have compared to many people in the world who have very little.

3. What can we do to keep a healthy perspective on material things? How can we, on a daily basis, maintain an attitude that we have daily bread and much more?

The Countercultural Call to Contentment

Contentment, in many circles, is equivalent to being lazy, unmotivated, and even unpatriotic! In a culture where upgrading your computer, car, and clothing are considered normal and desirable behavior, contentment is the enemy. Most of us are predisposed to want more and more. Then, when we get what we were dreaming about, we often want even more.

Into our pathologically greedy world, Jesus teaches, "Pray for what you need — for your daily bread." Such an idea begins to make sense only when we seek to live with contentment. This is the discipline of simplicity, the process of learning to say one powerful word, "Enough!" As we learn to enjoy what we have and not always strive for more, contentment grows in our hearts. As that happens, our daily bread starts to look like what we really need. And it even tastes better.

Read 1 Timothy 6:6 – 10 and Philippians 4:10 – 13

4. What does the apostle Paul warn about being discontent and always wanting more?

How is contentment presented in a positive light in these passages?

5. Name some mind-sets and attitudes in our culture that push us away from living a truly contented life.

6. Take a moment to write down some of the material things God has provided for you:

   • Where you live

   • Your transportation

   • Toys and fun stuff

- Tools and things that help you do your work

- Furniture and appliances

- Other things

Think of daily bread representing the basics of life, what you really need (not all of your wants). How might your life change or look different if you experienced inner contentment?

Authentic Thankfulness

Parents say it over and over and over through the childhood years as they raise their little boy or girl. "What do you say?" they ask. They are looking for a very specific answer, just two little words: "Thank you!" Of course, they also want their son or daughter to really mean it. But, for now, just hearing it would be a good start.

God has given his children daily bread and, in many cases, so much more. When we learn to say "Thank you," he is delighted. One of the ways we can honor God is by praying for our daily bread and actually thanking God when we get it. Think about the parent who has asked their child, "What do you say?" countless times over the years. Then, one day, their daughter just says it. "Thank you!" She was not coaxed or prodded, and Dad or Mom can tell by the look in her eyes that she really means it. What a day that is for a parent! In the same way, God waits for his children to come to a place of authentic and natural thanks.

Read James 1:16 – 18; Ephesians 5:1 – 20; and Psalm 100

7. Why is thankfulness so important in the life of a follower of Jesus?

What do we declare to God and the world when we live with authentic thankfulness for our daily bread?

8. How has God provided daily bread (or more) for you?

Sharing Our Bread

Jesus did not teach us to pray, "Give *me* today *my* daily bread." He said to pray for *our* daily bread. He wants us to be concerned not only about what *I* need, but what *we* need. All through the Bible we see that God's heart beats for those in need. If we see with the eyes of God, feel with his heart, and serve with his hands, we will also care about those who have no daily bread. We will actually be willing to joyfully share the bread we have with those who have none.

Read 1 John 3:16 – 18; Matthew 25:31 – 36; and Luke 12:32 – 34

9. How have you experienced the sharing of daily bread accomplishing *one* of the following?

- ☐ Reminding you that all of your bread is a gift from God
- ☐ Showing others in God's family that they are loved and that he wants to provide for them
- ☐ Revealing to spiritual seekers that God's compassion and love is alive in the hearts of his followers

10. What are some ways the local church can engage more intentionally in sharing daily bread with people in your community?

11. What one specific way could you take another step forward in sharing your daily bread with people in need?

Celebrating and Being Celebrated

In question six you listed some of the things God has provided for you. Take time to offer prayers of thanks for God's loving supply of daily bread and so much more.

Loving and Being Loved

Often we try to protect young people from the harsh realities of this world. If we have plenty of daily bread, we are afraid to let them see, with their own eyes, people who struggle each day just to survive. Consider taking a child, a niece, a nephew, or even a class of young people from your church to serve at a local mission or shelter. You will need to contact the organization first to make sure they are ready for your visit.

Use this as a springboard to talk about things like:

• How much we have
• The real needs in the world
• What it means to have "nothing to eat" or "nothing to wear"
• How we can share our bread with others
• Other questions that come up

Serving and Being Served

If you want to create a regular opportunity to share your daily bread and have your perspective adjusted, consider supporting a child through World Vision, Compassion International, or another relief agency. Keep a picture of this child on your refrigerator or even on your dining room table. Pray for them at meals. Read about their home country and how they live. If you have children or grandchildren, invite them to be part of this ministry by providing them a giving jar in which they can deposit donations.

Forgive Us Our Debts

MATTHEW 6:12, 14 – 15; 18:21 – 35

JESUS TAUGHT US TO PRAY, "FORGIVE US OUR DEBTS, AS WE ALSO HAVE FOR-given our debtors." What does it mean to *be* a debtor? What does it mean to *have* debtors? What is Jesus asking us to pray?

Maybe the simplest way to explain this is in the arena of finances. Let's say that you have borrowed money to buy a house and a car and have used a credit card to pay for gasoline, groceries, and clothing. Who is expected to pay the monthly mortgage or payment? The basic rule of society can be summed up quite clearly: You owe ... you pay! It is a rare thing indeed to have someone else offer to pay off your debt. You are a debtor, and the bank wants their money.

If you are not sure how this rule works, feel free to test it out. Go to your bank and ask to chat with a bank officer. Express your feelings honestly: "This debt that I carry is just too much for me. It's hampering my lifestyle. It is hard to pay these bills every month. In fact, paying back the money I owe you is getting a bit depressing. So, I think I'll quit. Are you comfortable with my choice?"

You'll likely discover that people who lend money are quite touchy about the whole "paying it back" thing. They keep very careful accounts of what is owed to their institution. If you fail to pay back a bank, you will learn that they have a whole team of people ready to help you realize the importance of repaying your debt. If you borrow from a less reputable institution, they sometimes have people on the payroll who will make a personal visit and do whatever it takes to get the money you owe. There is an aquatic animal metaphor for a person who loans money and collects by using strong mea-sures. We call that person not a guppy, a goldfish, or a clown fish ... but a loan *shark*. They know the rule: You owe ... you pay.

In this prayer, Jesus is addressing another kind of debt. It is the debt of sin and moral failure. The truth is, each one of us has a mountain of moral debt we can't pay off. It is a debt against God and other people. We also know that others have sinned against us and they can't pay their debt either. Each one of us has been the perpetrator of sin and the victim of sin. We have debtors and we are debtors.

As Jesus teaches us to pray, he calls us to ask God to forgive us as we forgive others. Charles Williams wrote, "No word in English carries a greater possibility of terror than the little word 'as' in that clause." Why? Because Jesus makes a correlation between the way I treat my debtors and the way God Almighty will treat me as a debtor.

Making the Connection

1. How have you experienced the rule "You owe ... you pay" in your financial life or in some other area of life?

Knowing and Being Known

Read Matthew 6:12, 14 – 15 and 18:21 – 35

2. Both these passages have a surprisingly harsh edge when it comes to the idea of forgiving others the way God has forgiven us. According to them, what is the connection between God's forgiveness toward us and the way we forgive others?

What kind of responses and emotions arise when you read these passages?

3. Imagine you are *one* of the characters in the Matthew 18 parable. From your perspective, what happened in the story and what should a reader of this parable learn? (Try to give your response in the first person ... as you believe that person would have responded.)

- ☐ The king
- ☐ The servant who was forgiven a great debt
- ☐ That same servant who would not forgive a small amount
- ☐ The other servants who stood at a distance and watched the drama unfold

You Owe ... You Pay

The parable in Matthew 18 seems to grow from a real-life situation. It appears that Peter has a debtor; someone has wronged him. Knowing that Jesus is big on the whole forgiveness thing, Peter asks if he should forgive up to seven times. This was over twice as many times as the rabbis would normally recommend. Jesus' response was staggering. He said we should forgive seventy-seven times (or seven times seventy). The point was that there should be no end to our forgiveness.

In the parable, the normal human system of economics (and forgiveness) is presented clearly. The servant owed a great debt and the time of payment came due. Because he could not pay his debt, he would face consequences and they would be severe. This would not surprise Jesus' listeners because they knew the rule: You owe ... you pay. The servant had a debt that was insanely large (bigger than the gross national product of the kingdom). He could not pay it. So, off to jail with him and his whole family.

Read Matthew 18:21–25

4. How would the king in the parable have been justified in doing all he could to get some of his money back from this man?

5. The king in the parable is a picture of God. Our sin against a perfect and holy God has created a debt bigger than we can imagine or dream. How would God be justified and fair if he decided to enforce the "You owe … you pay" rule?

You Owe … I Pay

The king in the parable is moved with compassion. Looking at the frightened, selfish, desperate, foolish servant, he's moved with pity. He does two things, and in the original text he does them in this order. First, he releases the man and his family — no prison, no torture, no forced labor … he lets him go. Next, he does the unthinkable; he forgives the debt. He wipes it away. First he removes the punishment and next he removes the debt.

The king forgives a mountain of debt, a huge sum of money. And the debt doesn't just disappear. Somebody has to pay, and it's the king himself. He offers a whole new system of debt management: You owe … I'll pay. This is the economy of grace. The king says, "I will pay the unpayable debt. I will take the hit. I will suffer the loss. I will take the whole price on myself so you can go free. You owe … I'll pay."

This is really a story about the human race. This is our story. Jesus says there is a king — there is a God — who is lavishly generous and painstakingly just. Human beings have accumulated a mountain of unpayable moral debt because of our sins. But the king comes and says, "You owe … I'll pay." It cost him the life of his beloved Son. It cost him the best he had, and he paid it without hesitation. That is grace. That is debt-canceling at its best.

Read Matthew 18:26 – 27 and Colossians 2:13 – 15

6. How does the cross of Jesus act as the ultimate debt repayment in human history?

Think about your own mountain of moral debt that Jesus canceled through his sacrifice on the cross. How are you like the forgiven servant in this story?

7. In light of all that followers of Jesus have been forgiven, how should we treat people who have sinned against us (our debtors)?

You Owe ... I Won't Forgive

In act two of this parable, the freshly forgiven and newly debt-free servant encounters a man who owes him some money. The debt is really just lunch money compared to the millions he has been forgiven. The debtor pleads for patience and time to pay him back.

Jesus' listeners would expect the radically forgiven servant to extend the same grace and debt-erasing plan to a fellow servant. Instead, the story takes a bizarre twist. The man who had been forgiven a king's ransom refused to forgive someone else the lunch money they owed. Imagine the shock of Jesus' listeners to learn that the man who was saved by grace showed no compassion. He actually grabbed the debtor by the throat in a gesture of violence and contempt, and demanded to be paid back. This recipient of an ocean of grace would not offer a thimble of forgiveness to someone else!

Read Matthew 18:28 – 30

8. At this point in Jesus' story, what kind of feelings and emotions do you think he was seeking to evoke in the hearts of his listeners?

9. What are some examples of how we can be just like the unforgiving servant in this story?

How do you think God feels about people who have been forgiven all of their sins and yet still refuse to extend grace to others?

Read Matthew 6:12, 14 – 15 and 18:31 – 35

10. Even when we know this story and the spiritual truth being communicated, it is still hard to forgive. What keeps us from forgiving others a comparatively small debt, even when we know God has forgiven us an infinitely larger debt?

He Paid ... I Must Forgive

The final act in the drama of this parable is painful to watch. We discover that this is a tragedy. The first servant is brought before the king, but this time there are no tears, no pleadings, and no bargains. The king says to the slave (a loose paraphrase), "You didn't get it at all, did you? It didn't penetrate. You have badly misunderstood me, my friend. You thought grace meant I was a fuzzy-minded incompetent and that I would let you get away with whatever you wanted and abuse whomever you chose. You used my grace as an excuse to be the same old, hurtful, self-centered, unforgiving person you were before. You were shown forgiveness, but you won't give it. You were granted mercy, but you won't bestow it. You were showered with love, but you won't extend it at all. You were offered the economy of grace, and you've chosen the economy of vengeance. Have it your way."

This moment in the parable unveils a sobering reality. When we know that God has paid the price for all of our sins through Jesus Christ, we are expected to live in his debtor-forgiveness plan. It is no longer a moment-by-moment choice. It is now an expectation. He paid ... I must forgive.

11. Without using names, recount a personal story about *one* of the following:

☐ How you extended grace and forgiveness to someone, living in God's debt-reduction plan

☐ A time when you did not forgive someone else and how this impacted you, your relationship with God, or your relationship with others

☐ A situation where someone refused to forgive you and the consequences of this unforgiveness

Celebrating and Being Celebrated

Read the following passages:

- 1 Corinthians 15:3
- 2 Corinthians 5:16–21
- Colossians 2:13–15
- 1 Peter 3:18
- Revelation 1:4–6

Spend time in prayer celebrating the gift Jesus offered when he died on the cross in your place to cancel the debt of your sins.

Loving and Being Loved

God's ultimate act of love was a sacrifice. He paid a price so that he could extend forgiveness to his lost, broken, and undeserving children. We are called to be part of this same debt-reduction plan. Make a list of people you have not yet been able to forgive (their debt against you could be small or quite large). Then, begin to ask God for the strength, courage, and awareness of his grace that is needed to extend forgiveness. One by one, take the life-giving step of forgiving each individual.

Serving and Being Served

Ephesians 4:15 (NIV 1984) says: "Instead, speaking the truth in love, we will in all things grow up into him who is the Head, that is, Christ."

Because the call of Jesus to forgive is so clear and because the consequences of ignoring this call are so severe, we are propelled forward on our journey of forgiveness. At the same time, we can invite others along. When we encounter followers of Jesus who say things like, "I will never forgive him," or "I don't think I will ever be able to forgive what she did to me," we should be prepared to speak the truth in love. The business of forgiveness is for everyone who follows Jesus. It should mark our lives. The world should look on in awe! Be bold in sharing this critical and often neglected calling with others. As you do, it will help you to be more intentional about growing as one who forgives your debtors.

Deliver Us from the Evil One

MATTHEW 6:13; 1 CORINTHIANS 10:6 – 13

WE WERE HAVING DINNER AT THE HOME OF FRIENDS. IT WAS A BEAUTIFUL evening so we were eating outside. Every so often I'd hear a strange sound, a kind of electric "zap." Finally my curiosity got the best of me and I asked, "What's that zapping sound?" "Oh, it's the sound of bugs hitting our bug zapper," they said, and went on to describe the gadget that attracted insects with its light, only to sizzle them when they got too close. It went on all night long — bug after bug — hundreds of bugs. "Zap! Zap! Zap!"

I must admit that this experience got me trying to think like a bug. You'd think that an approaching bug might observe the tray underneath the zapping light filled with hundreds of dead bugs and wonder, "Is this a good idea?"

Only a bug could possibly be that dense, right? Only a bug would go flying mindlessly into the same trap that countless other bugs have died in, right? Well, let's think about the glowing light of temptation that the evil one places in front of human beings. Listen closely and you will hear it. Political leaders. "Zap!" Pastors and church leaders. "Zap!" Successful business leaders. "Zap!" Wealthy athletes. "Zap!" Homemakers. "Zap!" Construction workers, televangelists, school teachers. "Zap! Zap! Zap!" It never seems to end.

Ever since Eve saw that the fruit of the tree was good for food and pleasing to the eye and desirable for wisdom, "Zap!" Over and over we read and hear of people who fall into temptations that devastate their lives, destroy their marriages, rock their worlds, break up their families, and wither their souls. Why do we voluntarily give in to what we know is going to be destructive? Why do we fly into the light?

The Bible teaches that we have an enemy who is bigger, stronger, and smarter than us. He is devoting time, investing energy, and marshaling the forces of hell in an effort to draw us into sin. This is why the Bible is filled with warnings about the evil one:

> Finally, be strong in the Lord and in his mighty power. Put on the full armor of God, so that you can take your stand against the devil's schemes. For our struggle is not against flesh and blood, but against the rulers, against the authorities, against the powers of this dark world and against the spiritual forces of evil in the heavenly realms. (Ephesians 6:10–12)

> Be alert and of sober mind. Your enemy the devil prowls around like a roaring lion looking for someone to devour. (1 Peter 5:8)

> "You belong to your father, the devil, and you want to carry out your father's desires. He was a murderer from the beginning, not holding to the truth, for there is no truth in him. When he lies, he speaks his native language, for he is a liar and the father of lies." (John 8:44)

> "And lead us not into temptation, but deliver us from the evil one." (Matthew 6:13)

Making the Connection

1. Imagine you are a military commander expected to brief the troops on the enemy they will be fighting: Satan. What would you tell them about the tactics he uses to lure people into sin?

Knowing and Being Known

Read 1 Corinthians 10:6 – 13

Three Keys in the Battle Against Temptation

First Corinthians 10:6 – 13 is a synopsis of the sins into which the people of Israel were lured while they wandered the desert for forty years following their escape from Egypt. Some of these sins were repeated over and over again: idolatry, immorality, testing God, grumbling. After this brief history of one of Israel's low points, the apostle Paul identifies three truths to give hope and encouragement to those facing temptation.

1. *Temptation will come to everyone; expect it.* This is not meant to discourage us; just the opposite. We are not alone. Every follower of Jesus will face temptation. Even Jesus was tempted (Matthew 4:1 – 11). Of course, he did not give in and commit sin. But if the evil one tried to tempt Jesus himself, we had better believe he will come after us as well. When we let this truth sink into our hearts and lives, we will be ever vigilant and watching out for places the enemy might seek to attack. This preparedness becomes a weapon to resist the devil.

2. *God will not let us be tempted beyond what we can handle.* There is no temptation we will face that is not first filtered through the Father's eyes and caring hands. God is faithful and will not allow the enemy to tempt us beyond our ability to resist. This truth brings hope, but it is also sobering. We can never rationalize our sin by saying, "I couldn't help myself. I just couldn't resist any further." God knows what we can handle and will never allow us to be tempted beyond what we can stand against . . . in his power.

3. *God will provide a way of escape.* When temptation comes, we need to look around. There is always a way out. We might have to run or we might have to fight. It could be a big "No!" or the exercise of Spirit-led self-control, but there is always a way out.

2. How does each of the truths in 1 Corinthians 10:13 bring hope and strength to followers of Jesus when we are facing temptation?

3. What is one area of temptation you are facing in your life today, and what are some possible "ways out" that God has provided?

The Strength of Joy

In the rest of this session we will be looking at three specific actions that we can take to find a way out of temptation and the cycle of sin. If I had to name the single greatest emotional resource against temptation in one word, it would be the word *joy*. The first way out of temptation is to arrange your life around joy. Set up your life so that you can experience high levels of the joy of the Lord.

What we often forget is that joylessness is always a setup for vulnerability to sin and disobedience. One writer puts it like this: "Failure to attain a deeply satisfying life always has the effect of making sinful actions seem good." Our success in overcoming temptation will be easier if we are joy-filled.

Read Nehemiah 8:10

4. How could joy in *one* of the following areas act as a deterrent to temptation?

☐ In the workplace

☐ In your marriage

☐ In how you use your resources

☐ In your family life

☐ In how you serve among God's people

5. What actions, decisions, and lifestyle choices have you found that help to unleash lasting joy in your heart?

6. What are the big joy-busters that tend to come in and drive you toward joylessness?

What can you do to avoid these joy-stealing situations?

The Wisdom of Accountability

The second way out of temptation that God provides is developing relationships of accountability. Temptation always involves keeping things hidden in the darkness. When we humbly tell trusted friends about our areas of struggle with sin, a light begins to shine and the power of sin begins to die. The enemy wants us to keep our sins, struggles, and temptations in the dark and to ourselves. He wants us to say in the quiet of our heart, "I can handle this on my own. I don't need to tell anyone else about this. It would be better if no one ever knew about my sin." The problem is, we have an enemy who is stronger and smarter than we are. Thankfully, God is infinitely stronger and smarter than the evil one. If we try to fight on our own, we are bound to lose. We need to invite God and God's people into the process.

Read James 5:16

7. What are some of Satan's lies and deceptions that make us fearful to tell others about our temptations and sins?

What are some legitimate reasons people are apprehensive about sharing the dark places of their sin and temptation?

8. How can we press past the lies and the legitimate concerns and move to a place of authentic and faith-strengthening accountability?

The Sword of the Spirit

Another way out of temptation God offers is the power of the Bible. There is amazing strength in knowing and following the Word of God. When the tempter came to Jesus at the beginning of his ministry (see Matthew 4; Luke 4), the weapon Jesus used over and over was the truth of Scripture. Once, twice, three times the evil one tempted him. Each time Jesus countered by quoting the Bible, "It is written." Jesus' mind was so washed in the Word, and he lived in its reality so thoroughly, that he saw right through Satan's deceptions.

Too often we consider memorizing verses or sections of the Bible as an exercise for children so they can get a gold star on a chart. Jesus saw the Word of God as a powerful weapon against the enticements of the devil. Like a sword, he could wield this weapon with great effectiveness. If we are in a spiritual battle — and we are — then it is time for us to sharpen the sword and get ready to fight back.

Read Matthew 4:1 – 11; Hebrews 4:12; and Ephesians 6:17

9. What do you learn from Jesus' use of Scripture, and how can you emulate his battle tactics?

10. Describe a time when you faced temptation and Scripture became your weapon to resist the enticements of the enemy.

11. What personal disciplines can you put in place to help you dig deeply into the Bible and meditate on the truth of God's Word?

Celebrating and Being Celebrated

In this session we have looked honestly and soberly at the reality that the devil is a formidable enemy. But we also have been reminded that God's power in us is far greater than the influence of the enemy. Reflect on the passages below, and then celebrate in prayer the power and victory we have in Jesus:

> You, dear children, are from God and have overcome them, because the one who is in you is greater than the one who is in the world. (1 John 4:4)

> And I saw an angel coming down out of heaven, having the key to the Abyss and holding in his hand a great chain. He seized the dragon, that ancient serpent, who is the devil, or Satan, and bound him for a thousand years. (Revelation 20:1–2)

> Submit yourselves, then, to God. Resist the devil, and he will flee from you. Come near to God and he will come near to you. (James 4:7–8)

Loving and Being Loved

Joy is one of the "ways out" that God provides when we are facing temptation. Take time in prayer to ask God to help you identify someone in your
life who is lacking joy. Commit to finding a way to be a joy-bearer in their
life. As you seek to bring joy to this person, pray that it will fortify them to
resist temptation and remain faithful to God's call on their life.

Serving and Being Served

One of the best gifts you can give to another follower of Jesus is to be a
person of such character that they can trust you to keep them accountable.
Take time to reflect on how trustworthy you are. Are you able to keep confi-
dences? Will you pray faithfully? Will you be a partner at their side as they
engage in spiritual warfare? When you feel you are ready, offer yourself as
an accountability partner to a close Christian friend.

Yours Is the Kingdom and the Power and the Glory

MATTHEW 6:9 – 13

HUMAN BEINGS HAVE A KINGDOM PROBLEM. WE THINK, "EVERYTHING IS ABOUT my kingdom, my power, and my glory." One of the best commentaries I know on this complex topic is a book on political science theory by a theologian named Dr. Seuss. The book is called *Yurtle the Turtle*. My parents read it to me when I was growing up, and I read it to my children.

It's a story about a little pond filled with little turtles that were ruled, or so he thinks, by a king named Yurtle. One day Yurtle the turtle king decides that his kingdom needs extending. "I'm king," he said, "of all I see. But I don't see enough. That's the trouble with me." So he began to stack turtles up to make himself a turtle throne.

The king lifts his finger and a whole pond of turtles scramble to obey, first dozens and then hundreds. They all exist for his sake, his kingdom, his power, and his glory. Atop his throne at last, he can see for miles. "I am Yurtle the turtle, oh marvelous me, for I am the ruler of all that I see."

Yurtle thinks his throne is as secure as a throne could be. And I suppose in a way it was. But in the end, his throne turns out to be a turtle tower of Babel. "And the turtle on the bottom did a plain little thing. He burped. And that burp shook the throne of the king. And today that great Yurtle, that marvelous he, is king of the mud. That's all he can see." This is how self-made thrones always end up. They can be human thrones, turtle thrones, or any kind of throne. If it is not the throne of God, it will always collapse and end up in the mud.

Jesus said, "So the last will be first, and the first will be last," and, "For those who exalt themselves will be humbled, and those who humble themselves will be exalted" (Matthew 20:16; 23:12). This is biblical truth. It's just the way things are in God's kingdom. We are wise to learn this lesson and commit ourselves to God's kingdom, power, and glory. We can try to build our own kingdoms, stack some turtles, and put ourselves first, but Jesus invites us to a life focused on his kingdom, his power, and his glory.

Making the Connection

1. What are some of the "turtle thrones" we build to exalt ourselves and make us look bigger than we really are?

   What are some of the little "burps" that can cause these human thrones to come tumbling down?

Knowing and Being Known

Read the Lord's Prayer as printed below:

> Our Father in heaven,
> hallowed be your name
> your kingdom come,
> your will be done
> on earth as it is in heaven.
> Give us today our daily bread.
> Forgive us our debts,
> as we also have forgiven our debtors.
> And lead us not into temptation,
> but deliver us from the evil one.
>
> For yours is the kingdom and the power and the glory forever.
>   Amen.

Yours Is the Kingdom

Like it or not, we are little kingdom builders. We want to make our families, work, friends, and sometimes even our churches into little kingdoms under our control. We want life to be about our agendas, our wants, and our needs. Some people are bold and obvious about this and others are stealthy and subtle. But we all have the same problem.

Jesus is inviting us to recognize, every day, that another kingdom is at work in this world that may not be as visible or look as impressive to human eyes or seem as urgent. But it is the most important kingdom of all. We may wonder from time to time whether God's kingdom is going to be the last kingdom standing, but it will be. So we pray, "Your kingdom, not my kingdom." In these words we express humble surrender.

2. When you get involved in "personal kingdom" building projects, how can this impact *one* of the following areas of your life?

   ☐ Your vocation
   ☐ Your friendships
   ☐ Your relationship with God
   ☐ Your marriage or parenting
   ☐ Your use of personal resources
   ☐ Some other aspect of your life

3. What have you discovered that helps you keep your mind, heart, and energy focused on God's kingdom building projects and off personal kingdom pursuits?

Yours Is the Power

When we rely on our power, we always come up short. When we pray, "Yours is the power," we discover that God can supply all we need. It seems upside down, but this is how things work in God's kingdom. Ask yourself a few questions: Do I need power in my life? Do I face challenges at work I can't seem to manage? Are there places and situations in this world I am concerned about? Do I lack the strength needed to restore and heal a broken relationship? Do I have a friend or family member who needs power beyond what they can muster? Do I struggle with worry, fear, or concerns that keep me up at night? If you said yes to any of these questions, the answer is *not* to try harder. It is *not* to pull yourself up by your spiritual bootstraps. The answer is to admit, "I can't do it. I lack the power to make these things right." When we come to this point, we can cry out, "Yours is the power," and things will begin to turn around.

Read Acts 12:1 – 11, 18 – 19, 21 – 24

4. This account in Acts captures an epic example of how human power and God's power are radically different. What do you learn about human power in this passage and what do you learn about God's power?

5. We all face situations in this life in which we lack the power and strength to make it through on our own. Tell about when you faced a situation like this, cried out for God's power, and he brought you through.

How do you think this situation would have turned out if you had insisted on pressing forward in your own strength?

6. Where do you need God's sustaining power today?

How can Christian friends pray for you, encourage you, and even be conduits of God's power as you face this situation?

Yours Is the Glory

It is possible to cry out, "Yours is the kingdom! Yours is the power! And mine is the glory!" When God's kingdom is breaking into our lives and when his power is flowing, the evil one will entice us to take the credit and try to get the glory. We must battle this temptation toward pride and self-glorification. The antidote is passionate worship. When we are on our knees in prayer, lifting up our voices in worship, or pointing to God and declaring, "To God be the glory," it is hard to be consumed with pride.

Read Psalms 34:1 – 3; 63:3 – 4; and 86:12 – 13

7. When we are humbly honest, only God deserves to be glorified and lifted up in worship. What are some reasons that God deserves glory (and we do not)?

God Is: **We Are:**

8. It is easy to give God glory and praise when we gather for worship services with other Christ followers. But if we are going to live a "Yours is the glory" lifestyle, it will mean worshiping God all through the week. What are some of the ways you keep your heart, lips, and mind filled with worship in the flow of an ordinary day?

Every Knee Will Bow

In our world, God's name is not always hallowed. Countless times every day, the name of God is used by one human being to curse another; so too is the name of Jesus thrown around and treated in profane ways. But one day the true King will lift his finger, and a whole lot of thrones that seem real secure will come tumbling down. A whole lot of big turtles are going to end up flipped on their backs — stuck in the mud with their little feet waving in the air. The Bible tells us that a time will come when "every knee will bow."

How many knees will bow? Every knee! Try to picture the scene. All humanity, every person from Adam until the very end of time, will bow in acknowledgment of the supremacy of Jesus. Every president who ever lived, every king and queen, every CEO, every movie star, every billionaire ... everyone will bow down. Even those who refused to bow the knee in life: Hitler, Stalin, Caesar Augustus, Herod ... every knee will bow!

Read Philippians 2:1–11

9. How do you see both the humility and glory of Jesus in this passage?

10. One way we bow our knees to Jesus in this life is by humbly following his will revealed in the Bible. In this passage the apostle Paul gives a number of exhortations:

    ☐ Be like-minded, having the same love, being one in spirit and purpose (a call to unity).

    ☐ Do nothing out of selfish ambition or vain conceit (a call to examine our motives).

    ☐ In humility consider others better than yourselves (a call to humility).

    ☐ Look not only to your own interests, but also to the interests of others (a call to service).

    How might you bow your knee in this life by following *one* of the exhortations listed above? Consider at least one practical action.

Celebrating and Being Celebrated

Lift up prayers of celebration in three ways:

- Celebrate God's kingdom as it breaks into this world.
- Rejoice in God's power as you relinquish your own.
- Declare God's glory by bowing your knees, lifting your voice, and giving him praise.

Loving and Being Loved

Take time in the coming week to meet with God on your knees. A day will come when every knee will bow, even those who refused to do so in this life. Meet with God on your knees and declare your love, your devotion, and your commitment to bend the knee regularly and willingly as his follower.

Serving and Being Served

His is the glory! Commit, in a fresh new way, to be a passionate worshiper both in your private life and when you gather with God's family. Purpose in your heart that you will give God praise and glory. Commit to him that you will not just show up for worship, but you will engage yourself fully. Let this be your act of service to the God to whom you say, "Yours is the kingdom and the power and the glory."

THE
PRINCIPLES
of JESUS

Bill Hybels

An Audience of One

MATTHEW 6:1 – 18

I WAS WATCHING A CHICAGO BEARS FOOTBALL GAME RECENTLY WHEN I MENtioned that a running back made a move like Walter Payton. Half of the people in the room looked at me and said, "Walter who?" I couldn't believe it! It was not that many years ago that Walter Payton was a household name for anyone who watched even a little professional football. At that moment I was struck by the stark reality that the applause of the masses is both fickle and fleeting.

Orienting our lives around pleasing other people is a guaranteed setup for dissatisfaction, disillusionment, and major disappointment. Against this brief backdrop, listen to this one single sentence from the greatest sermon in the world, the Sermon on the Mount: Jesus said, "Be careful not to practice your righteousness in front of others to be seen by them. If you do, you will have no reward from your Father in heaven" (Matthew 6:1). In this single sentence Jesus seeks to spare you and me from a lifetime and maybe even an eternity of disillusionment and dissatisfaction. He wants all of his followers to be attentive to something strangely human: the tendency in all of us to want to please other people.

This desire to please other people seems to kick into high gear when it comes to matters of faith. Jesus tells us that if we are not careful, it is possible to spend years attending Christian events and church services, singing Christian songs, doing Christian deeds, and obeying Christian rules and end up with only human congratulations but no divine affirmation. In other words, Jesus wants us to be careful not to trade his blessing and kingdom for a few handshakes and pats on the back!

What is really important in life and eternity is that we please God. Our lives should be about seeking his approval and affirmation, not human praise. In other words, we should live our lives to an audience of One!

Making the Connection

1. Tell about a time when you were drawn to please and impress people rather than live for God. Pick *one* of the areas suggested below:

   ☐ In your childhood   ☐ In the workplace

   ☐ In your teen years   ☐ In your church

   What resulted from your people-pleasing activities?

Knowing and Being Known

Read Matthew 6:1 – 18

2. In the first verse of this passage, Jesus gives a primary truth under which the whole rest of the passage stands. Use the space below to put this truth in your own words.

3. In light of what Jesus teaches in this passage, how do you think Jesus would respond to these statements (choose *one*)?

   ☐ "I would like to give a special gift to the church, but I would like some kind of a modest recognition such as a plaque with my name on it or an acknowledgment in the church newsletter."

☐ "I'm a little tired today. You see, the Lord has called me to wake up extra early so I can spend a good hour every morning in prayer."

☐ "I just love to fast. It cleanses my body and I feel so close to God during these times. As a matter of fact, I am committed to fasting for three days every month. Have you made this kind of spiritual commitment in your life?"

4. In this passage, Jesus gives a serious warning in three areas of spiritual discipline. What are the dos and don'ts for each area of Jesus' teaching?

When you *give*:
Do ...

Don't ...

When you *pray*:
Do ...

Don't ...

When you *fast*:
Do ...

Don't ...

Why do you think Jesus is so serious about how we live out our lives of faith?

Motive Check

Jesus goes right to the heart on this matter. Part of the reason Jesus alerts his listeners to this propensity to live out faith for human applause is that he knows what he's going to talk about next. In the next part of the Sermon on the Mount, Jesus is going to be talking about giving money to kingdom causes. He minces no words in challenging people that giving money to Christian causes is a part of what it means to be a Christian. Jesus is also going to talk about the importance and power of prayer, and about spiritual disciplines such as fasting (denying yourself food for a time to really concentrate on spiritual development). But before he launches into these topics, Jesus wants his listeners to do a motive check. "Why are you doing what you're doing?" he asks. "And for whom are you doing it?" Jesus knows that if he begins talking about giving money, praying, and fasting, people might wind up doing these things for all the wrong reasons. Many spiritual activities can be done for recognition from others, and if that is our motive, we will have no reward from our Father in heaven. Jesus is deeply concerned about what drives and motivates each of us in our spiritual life.

5. What are some signals or signs that a person is motivated by his or her desire to impress people and not a desire to please God?

6. We all need to slow down on occasion and assess our motives. Use the graphs that follow to honestly evaluate what is motivating you in your spiritual life:

What motivates me . . .

In my *church attendance*

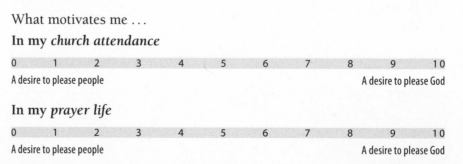

0   1   2   3   4   5   6   7   8   9   10
A desire to please people   A desire to please God

In my *prayer life*

0   1   2   3   4   5   6   7   8   9   10
A desire to please people   A desire to please God

In my *giving*

0	1	2	3	4	5	6	7	8	9	10

A desire to please people   A desire to please God

In my *service* in the church

0	1	2	3	4	5	6	7	8	9	10

A desire to please people   A desire to please God

Now consider one area in which you feel God is calling you to please him more. Invite your Christian friends to pray for you to have pure motives as you grow in this area of your spiritual life.

The Law of Compensation

If you spend forty to fifty hours a week plugging away at IBM, you don't go over to Hewlett Packard on Friday afternoon to get your paycheck. The marketplace rule is that you expect to be paid by the one for whom you're working. This is a simple law of compensation.

It's the same with the kingdom law of compensation. You receive your payment or reward from the One for whom you work. If the primary reason you do spiritual stuff is to make your spouse, kids, parents, or pastor happy, then your reward will come from them. Jesus says, "If that is your motivation, you will get a reward, but it won't be from me." All Jesus is saying is that when your spouse, parent, pastor, or friend gives you that pat on the back, that's your payday. Don't expect any more!

Jesus says that the real tragedy in working for the praise of people is not so much in what we get from them but what we *don't* get from the Father. Human applause is fickle and fleeting, but the blessing of the Father lasts forever! You don't want to miss his rewards or compensation because they are rich and soul-satisfying. Jesus wants us to get the best compensation possible, so he tells us to be sure we are working for our heavenly Father and not for other people.

7. What are some of the rewards we get when we live our lives to please people?

8. What are some of the rewards we get when we live our lives to please God?

How are God's rewards different than the world's praise and rewards?

A Sober Warning

The Bible teaches that we will all appear before God someday to give an account of our life — no exceptions. Jesus says when that day comes, some people are going to stand before the Lord so proud of their church attendance, their giving record, and how often they prayed only to be shocked when they hear God the Father say, "Depart from me. I don't even know who you are." Translated, this means, "You weren't doing all of that stuff for me; you were doing it for human applause. You have already received your reward. Depart from me because none of what you did had anything to do with me." Jesus wants to spare you and me from that. We matter too much for him not to warn us of this potential tragedy.

Read Matthew 7:21 – 23

9. What kind of response do you think Jesus was looking for when he spoke these words?

What is your first response when you read these words of Jesus?

10. How does this warning motivate you in *one* of the following areas of your life?

☐ Your heart to share the love of Jesus with those who are not his followers

☐ The need to evaluate your own faith and what motivates you to do "spiritual things"

☐ The need to encourage friends and family members to be authentic in their faith

Celebrating and Being Celebrated

People who genuinely orient their lives around pleasing God are those who have had unforgettable experiences or encounters with God. People who jump through hoops, practice religious drills, and go around looking for spiritual pats on the back are not bad people; they just have never really known God personally. Maybe a biblical example would help make the point. The apostle Paul was first called Saul. Saul was intensely religious, but he did not know God. He was a people pleaser to the core. He was always asking, "What do the teachers want me to do, what do the rabbis want me to do, what would impress the religious leaders and elevate me in their sight?" Do you know one of the first questions Paul asked God after his conversion? "Lord, what would *you* have me do?" Now Paul wanted to orient his whole life around living to an audience of One.

Close with a time of prayer—first, asking God's forgiveness for those times you are a people pleaser instead of a God pleaser; then, praising him that Jesus has given us a clear call to live our lives to an audience of One.

Loving and Being Loved

In the coming week, reflect on the people in your life who you feel are examples of pure motives in how they live their faith. Lift up prayers of thanks for these people who have been an example and encouragement to you. Give one or two of them a call, write a note, or send an email to let them know that God has used their example of pure motives to encourage you in your faith.

Serving and Being Served

Identify one act of care, love, or compassionate service that you can render for someone this week. Be sure no one knows about it; don't tell a single person about what you have done. Simply enjoy the satisfaction of knowing that you are living for an audience of One!

Secret Faith

MATTHEW 6:1 – 18

JESUS WANTED HIS LISTENERS TO BE VERY CLEAR ABOUT THE NEED FOR THEIR hearts to be changed, not just their behavior. Before he continued in his teaching, Jesus wanted them to do a motivation check and ask themselves the question, "Why am I doing what I'm doing?" Jesus wanted to make sure that their motives were right as they became inspired to grow more, give more, and pray more. It is the very same test that Jesus wants us to take. It is called "the secrecy test."

There are three questions in this secrecy test:

Question 1: How much money would you give to kingdom causes if the only one who ever knew about it was God? If a plate was never passed in church, if there was no one who knew what you gave, how much money would you joyfully give?

Question 2: How often would you pray if no one else was keeping track? If no one ever saw you, heard you, or even knew you were a person of prayer, would you still take time to seek God's face in prayer?

Question 3: How important would fasting be in your spiritual development if no one but God knew you were fasting? In Jesus' day, the religious leaders, in an attempt to show how spiritual they were, fasted publicly. They would walk around unshaven, with dirty hair and unlaundered robes, just so that people would know that they were fasting. They wanted others to look at them and be impressed with their spiritual devotion and sacrificial lifestyle.

This simple three-question secrecy test exposes motivations. It clarifies what you are doing for others and what you are doing out of a loving response to the God who loves you. It determines who's impressing others and who's seeking to live for an audience of One.

Making the Connection

1. Why do so many people have a hard time keeping a secret?

Why do you think people are quick to let others know about their religious accomplishments rather than keeping them private?

Knowing and Being Known

Read Matthew 6:1 – 4

2. According to Jesus, what is the proper spirit and approach to giving?

What warnings does Jesus give to people who feel called to share their material goods with those in need?

Secret Giving

I want to suggest five simple principles that should guide our giving, all of which are clearly taught in the Bible:

The Principle of Participation. God calls every one of his followers to participate in the joyous privilege of giving toward his work. He knows that if every Christian shared in this responsibility, there would be plenty of resources for all the work of the church. Jesus lets us know that the conversion of our heart is not complete until our wallet is open to kingdom causes (Matthew 6:21).

The Principle of Proportion. The Bible is clear that our giving should be in proportion to what God has given us. That is why God calls his followers to begin by giving the first 10 percent as a tithe toward his work (Malachi 3:10). This way, everyone can give generously, but we are not all giving the same amount (Luke 21:1 – 4).

The Principle of Joyfulness. Our giving should come from a willing spirit that takes joy in entering into the Lord's work through the giving of our gifts (2 Corinthians 9:7).

The Principle of Consistency. God wants us to develop a discipline of setting aside a portion of our income on a regular basis, such as weekly, biweekly, or monthly. This helps us stay on track with our giving and becomes a regular reminder of who has given us all we have (1 Corinthians 16:1 – 2).

The Principle of Anonymity. Finally, Jesus is very clear that we should be secret givers. We are not to use giving as an opportunity to impress people or posture for position in the church (Matthew 6:2 – 4).

3. What does it mean to announce your giving with trumpets, and how do some people do this today?

4. What are some practical ways we can keep our "left hand from knowing what our right hand is doing"?

Read Matthew 6:5 – 15

5. Jesus gives some general principles about how to pray and how not to pray. In light of what Jesus teaches in this passage, what warnings do you think Jesus would give you about how your prayer life can get off-track?

6. When Jesus gave the example of the Lord's Prayer, it was in the context of a very specific warning (Matthew 6:7 – 8). How can we use this prayer in ways that capture the spirit of what Jesus is teaching?

In light of Jesus' warning, what are some of the potential risks if we simply memorize this prayer and repeat it over and over again?

Secret Praying

Your character — who you are — is forged and shaped when no one is looking. Dwight L. Moody said, "Character is what you do in the dark." In this section of the Sermon on the Mount, Jesus is talking about true spiritual character. How are we living out our faith when no one is looking? Is it enough to know that the God who sees in secret will reward us? How often and how earnestly would we pray if only God were keeping track?

In Jesus' day, some defects had made their way into the prayer lives of some of his listeners. The primary defect was that prayer had become too public. Religious leaders liked praying in public places so that their prayers would be heard and noticed. They were often loud and theatrical so that people would not only see them but be impressed with them. Along with this, their prayers were becoming prescribed. Certain mechanical kinds of prayers were being said over and over and over again! The religious leaders of Jesus' day felt that if they followed a certain prayer pattern, God would have to listen to their prayers. They had come to believe that if they jumped through the right prayer hoops, they would get God's attention and be able to wrench a blessing out of his tight-fisted grip. These religious leaders were growing shallow and self-centered in their prayer lives, and Jesus wanted them to enter a more authentic and joy-filled place of prayer.

7. The Lord's Prayer is a springboard into many important areas we should focus on when we come before the Lord and talk with him. What are the key areas of life and faith Jesus teaches us to focus on when we pray?

8. In which of these areas do you need to spend more time in focused prayer?

How can your Christian friends join you in prayer as you go deeper in this area?

Secret Fasting

Why would God call us to abstain from food for a period of time? What does fasting have to do with prayer? Imagine you are facing a pressing decision in your life. Maybe you are in a painful relationship that you just can't seem to get out of. Perhaps you are facing a major trauma or are considering a big move in the workplace. You have a strong sense that the only way you are going to get through this time and gain clarity on how you should proceed is through prayer. So you go to work on Monday morning determined to pray about this issue often throughout the day. But as soon as you enter the workplace, the demands of the job begin to take over. Pretty soon, four or five hours have passed and you haven't prayed about your concern even one time. You began your day with the best intentions of praying, but you just couldn't pull it off because you got busy and lost your focus.

Now, add into this picture the dynamic of fasting. Several times during the course of the day you are going to want to eat, but every time your stomach growls, you pause for prayer instead. By the end of the day, you will have spent considerable time praying because your fasting has raised your awareness over and over again.

Read Matthew 6:16 – 18

9. If you have had an experience of fasting during a time of focused prayer, how did it impact your prayer life?

10. What is one pressing decision you need to make that you feel might call for a season of prayer and fasting?

Celebrating and Being Celebrated

Our giving is to be secret, but God's giving to us is lavish and public! He has poured out more blessings, joys, and good gifts than we can count. Lift up prayers of thanksgiving and celebration for the many things God has given you.

Loving and Being Loved

We can extend many acts of service and love to those we care about. However, few of them have more impact than the action of prayer. Make a list of two or three people whom you can commit to pray for every day for the next week. As you pray this coming week, keep your prayer secret — don't tell anyone! God knows, and that is enough.

Serving and Being Served

Think about those you know who are in a time of monetary need and pray about who God might want you to support. Provide something very practical (e.g., money for rent, a bag of groceries, a gift certificate for dinner out). Extend this act of service in secret and pray for God to get the praise.

The Truth about Treasures

MATTHEW 6:19 – 24

HAVING SPENT SOME TIME IN AIRPORTS, I HAVE HAD SOMETHING HAPPEN TO me on more than one occasion while walking down a narrow concourse. Maybe you have had a similar experience. While walking shoulder to shoulder with a mass of people you hear the sound of an oncoming golf cart. *Beep, beep, beep!* The golf cart is moving very quickly against the flow of traffic and does not seem to have a set of brakes. These babies don't often slow down. They operate under the "Moses effect" — they expect the crowd to part like the Red Sea as they beep their way through the ocean of people who have to walk from terminal to terminal.

As it approaches, you have a split-second decision to make: Are you going to dive off to the right or left side? You know this thing is coming through whether you move or not, so you jump out of the way as the golf cart flies past you.

From the beginning of the Sermon on the Mount, this is what Jesus does. He moves against the grain of the culture and divides the crowd in half, letting people know that they have to make a decision between two opposing worldviews. You can almost hear it — *beep, beep, beep!* — as Jesus moves through the crowd with the truth and people have to decide, *Will I jump to the right or to the left? Am I going to agree with Jesus or go my own way?*

As you read through the Sermon on the Mount, you will discover that Jesus draws clear lines in many areas of life and asks people to make a decision about where they will stand. One such area is how people view material things and the accumulation of wealth. Jesus had a lot to say about how they should handle earthly treasures. His Word is true for us today as well.

Making the Connection

1. Describe the perspective *one* of the following groups has about earthly treasures:

☐ Your nation   ☐ Your community   ☐ Your family

Knowing and Being Known

Read Matthew 6:19 – 24; Luke 12:16 – 21; and Ecclesiastes 2:4 – 11

2. Throughout the Bible we read many warnings about a life that is focused on consumption. What are some of the warnings you hear in these passages?

3. If a person ignores the warnings in these passages and lives a life centered on the accumulation of material things, what are some of the consequences he or she might experience?

4. Many of us have seen real-life examples of people who have spent their whole lives storing up treasures on earth. Think of one example and tell about how the pursuit of material wealth impacted this person's life.

Many of us have seen real-life examples of people who have spent their whole lives storing up treasures in heaven. Think of one example and tell about how the pursuit of spiritual wealth impacted this person's life.

Deposit #1: Worship

There are many ways we can make deposits in our spiritual bank accounts. For the remainder of this study we will look at some examples of how we can store up treasures in heaven. One joy-filled investment plan is the commitment to be a regular and passionate worshiper.

Worship is never wasteful in the eyes of God. Every act of private and corporate worship is a deposit in your heavenly bank account. Take time out on a regular basis to bow your head and sincerely acknowledge the goodness and grace of God. Find a moment to sing his praises. Pause with a friend and pray a prayer of thanks. Gather with God's people and celebrate his goodness! Not only does worship move and delight the heart of God, it helps to restore our perspective on what is truly valuable in this life.

Read Matthew 6:20 – 21

5. Jesus uses three images to warn us about the temporary nature of earthly treasures and the indestructible nature of heavenly treasures. What are these three images, and how do they help you understand the temporary nature of earthly treasures?

6. If Jesus were to sit down with you face-to-face as your eternal investment counselor, what do you think he would say about the value of investing in heavenly treasures?

7. Jesus said, "Where your treasure is, there your heart will be also." What are some indications that your heart is primarily about earthly things?

What are some indications that your heart is growing to be more and more focused on heavenly investments?

Deposit #2: Character Development

The Bible clearly teaches us that if we want to lay up treasure in heaven, one of the best investment strategies is personal character development. We should make every attempt to strengthen our character in a way that honors God. Each time we do this, it is a deposit in our heavenly bank account. This is expressed with crystal clarity in 1 Peter 3:8 – 9 with the words, "Finally, all of you, be like-minded, be sympathetic, love one another, be compassionate and humble. Do not repay evil with evil or insult with insult. On the contrary, repay evil with blessing, because to this you were called so that you may inherit a blessing."

Every time we choose love over hate, kindness over harshness, empathy over insensitivity, truth-telling over lying, forgiveness over grudge-bearing, a polite spirit over rudeness, silence over slander, wisdom over foolishness, purity over immorality, faith over fear, or generosity over stinginess, we delight the heart of God and add to our heavenly portfolio.

Read 1 Peter 3:8 – 12

8. There are many passages in the Bible that address the issue of character development. What specific areas does Peter focus on, and how can these areas function as investments in a heavenly bank account?

9. What is one area of character development you feel God is calling you to focus on?

How can your Christian friends pray for you, encourage you, and keep you accountable to grow in this area of character development?

Deposit #3: Expressions of Compassion

A young boy was walking on the beach after a huge tropical storm had washed up countless starfish on the shore. He knew that these little creatures would die if they stayed out of the water for too long, so this compassionate lad started throwing starfish back into the ocean. An elderly man was also walking along the beach that morning. He was a realist, and when he saw the boy attempting the seemingly impossible task of throwing all those starfish back into the water, he chuckled to himself. When his path crossed the path of the little boy, he commented, "You could do that all day, but I don't think you will make a difference." The boy looked at the man, picked up a starfish, threw it as far as he could into the ocean, and replied, "I think I made a difference for that one."

Every time we show an act of compassion, we build up our treasure in heaven. It might seem like a small act of kindness, but it counts! Others might look on and chuckle at our efforts. They might even say that we can't make a difference. But Jesus calls us to express his love, kindness, and compassion to those in need. When we do, we are storing up treasures in heaven where rust can't corrupt, moths can't eat, and thieves can't steal. It is a great investment plan!

10. What is one act of compassionate care and service you feel the Lord is calling you to offer to another person? (This can be a one-time act or participation in a regular ministry.)

11. If you are part of a small group, what is one ministry of compassion your group can take part in together in the coming month?

Celebrating and Being Celebrated

Because we live in a culture that spurs us on to want more and more, we often forget to stop and thank God for all we have. As you pray today, thank God for the way he has met your material needs. Be content with what he has given.

Loving and Being Loved

One of the greatest acts of love that we can extend to our heavenly Father is to worship him. Plan a time you can gather as a small group or with other Christian friends for a time of worship. If you or someone in your group can play piano, guitar, or another instrument, consider incorporating them. When you gather, spend time singing, praying, and sharing passages of Scripture that have helped you fall more in love with the Lord.

Serving and Being Served

In the final questions of this study you discussed a specific act of compassion and ministry that you or your small group can extend. Be sure to follow through on whatever you committed to do.

Why Worry?

MATTHEW 6:25 – 34

SOME YEARS AGO I HAD THE OPPORTUNITY TO HAVE DINNER WITH A MAN WHO owned a bungee-jumping company. We had some fascinating discussions about insurance premiums and the risks involved in this enterprise. I held my tongue for a while, but finally had to ask him if he had ever lost a customer. Thankfully, he had not!

One thing that did not surprise me was when he told me that almost all his customers feel fearful when they are standing up on the platform getting ready to jump with only a bungee cord to save them. He said that some people cover up their fear with acts and words of bravado. He also told me that no matter what they showed on the outside, pretty much everyone is afraid when standing up there for the first time. They want to experience the thrill of the long free fall, but there is another side of them that says they're terrified to jump off the edge and take the plunge.

Jesus knows about the universal reality of fear, and he addressed this topic in the Sermon on the Mount. My personal opinion is that Jesus brought up this subject in this particular part of the greatest sermon in history because he saw fear in the eyes of his listeners. Remember, Jesus had been talking about changing treasures. He had been saying that many of these people have oriented their lives around the acquisition and enjoyment of earthly treasures. He had called them to relax their grasp on their earthly treasures and firm up their grip on treasures that will last forever. Whenever you talk about relaxing your grip on earthly treasures, people become afraid.

This is still true today! Every time a pastor talks about changing treasures and about setting our focus on the things that will last forever, people get nervous, anxious, even fearful. I have taught these same truths to groups of people, and I have seen the fear in the eyes of those who were gathered.

In this passage, Jesus is encouraging us to trust the Father enough to take the dive into full devotion. He wants us to be able to enjoy the free fall and not be fearful about it. We don't need to worry. There are good reasons to trust the Father.

Making the Connection

1. Describe a time you stood on the ledge and had to make a leap of faith in *one* of the following areas:

   ☐ A literal jump like skydiving or bungee-jumping

   ☐ A step of faith to trust God for his provision or protection

   ☐ A relational jump in which you needed to trust another person to be there for you

   What happened after you took the jump?

Knowing and Being Known

Read Matthew 6:25 – 34

2. What are some of the real-life illustrations Jesus uses to help us realize we don't have to worry about our future but can trust our heavenly Father to take care of us?

3. In light of what Jesus teaches in this passage, imagine what he might say to someone making *one* of the following statements:

☐ God has forgotten me. I wonder if he knows the desperation of my situation.

☐ I wonder if God even cares about me. I can take care of myself.

☐ All I need to do is work harder, look out for number one, and be sure to protect my own interests. Then I will have what I need to make it through life.

You Are More Than a Body

Can you imagine a world-class heart surgeon spending twelve hours doing a meticulous heart transplant operation on a person, only to neglect the patient after surgery was over? Would the surgeon complete such a complex operation, sew the person up, and then neglect to order a bed, blankets, or postoperative care? Of course not! The surgeon says, "If I am doing all this work on your heart, you had better believe I am going to make sure you have a bed, some food, and fresh water to drink." Well, God is the Great Physician! He has healed you and given you a new heart! He is working a miracle of transformation inside of you. Do you really think he would fail to give you the daily food, drink, and clothing that you need?

Read Matthew 6:25 – 26

4. What are some life situations that cause you to be anxious and worried?

How do the words of Jesus speak to one of these situations?

5. Tell about a time when God surprised you with his provision. How does this experience help you trust him for your future needs?

You Are More Valuable Than Birds or Flowers

Another reason we can take a plunge of faith without anxiety about our future is that Jesus assures us that the Father takes care of birds and flowers. He wants us to know that we are much more valuable than either of these. First, Jesus uses a comparative approach from the animal kingdom. When is the last time you were walking and saw a bird in full flight run out of fuel and crash to the ground? Birds do just fine when it comes to the needed fuel of food and drink. They don't stockpile a lot of food; God gives them what they need each day. In a similar way, Jesus makes a comparison between flowers and people. Flowers last only a short time — hours, days or weeks — but then they are gone. People last so much longer and are so much more valuable than flowers. Surely, we can live with an expectation that God will provide for us.

Read Matthew 6:26, 28 – 30

6. Jesus makes a direct comparison between the lilies and King Solomon. How does this comparison give you hope concerning God's commitment to provide what you need?

7. Take a minute to make two brief lists:

Basic life needs God has provided for you	Basic life needs God has failed to provide for you

What do your lists tell you?

Worry Does Not Produce Positive Results

Another reason Jesus encourages us to stop worrying is that it does not produce anything of value. I wonder if Jesus is almost trying to lighten things up a little bit. He's asking people who worry a lot, "Just tell me about your life strategy here. When you commit yourself to the ministry of anxiety and worry, does it work? Can you manipulate events? Can you change things if you really worry hard?" The answer is obvious! Worry accomplishes nothing good or valuable. On the other hand, it does have many negative side effects. Jesus wants us to remember that our lives are in his hands. His care and provision are all we need, and worry will never accomplish his purposes.

Read Matthew 6:27

8. What are some potentially negative results of worry and anxiety?

9. What is one area of life in which you tend to worry? How can your Christian friends pray for you as you seek to offer this area to God and live in a trust-filled, worry-free manner?

You Have a Loving Father

One final reason we can take the plunge into a trust-filled lifestyle is that we have a Father in heaven who loves us more than we could ever dream. It makes perfect sense for people outside the family of God to fret and worry about their upcoming material needs because, in a very real sense, they are on their own in this world. They have rejected God's fathership and lordship over their lives. But Jesus has a powerful reminder for his followers: you are never alone in this world! You have a heavenly Father who loves you and will take care of you.

Read Matthew 6:31 – 34

10. Describe a time you saw a loving and caring parent provide for his or her son or daughter.

What did you learn about the character of this parent as you watched his or her provision, generosity, and tenderness?

11. As you reflect on God's provision in your life, what do you learn about his character and love for you?

Celebrating and Being Celebrated

We have all had times when we took a leap of faith and watched God catch us with his amazing provision and uphold us with his powerful protection. Lift up prayers celebrating God's rich provision and protection over your life.

Loving and Being Loved

God has instilled in each of us the need for community and care. He provides for this need through the close relationships and love of family and friends. Take time in the coming week to identify one or two people God has placed in your life to meet this need for community and care. Commit yourself to communicate with these people (by phone, in a letter, or over lunch) about how God has met some of the deepest needs in your life through them. Remind them of your love and God's love!

Serving and Being Served

One of the ways God provides for his children is through one another. Make a commitment to allow your resources to be used by God to provide for those who are in need. Establish a discipline in your life to pray each time you see a person in need. Ask God if he is prompting you to help that person. Remember, every need does not have to be met by you; however, as followers of Christ, we should always be ready for God to prompt our hearts to a place of willingness to give.

Judge Not

MATTHEW 7:1 – 5

SEVERAL YEARS AGO I WAS INVITED TO A WEDDING OF A CHURCH MEMBER. I was not officiating at the ceremony, so I came as a guest. I was looking forward to just being with the guests who had gathered in our chapel and enjoying the service.

As we were sitting and waiting for the ceremony to begin, I overheard two men directly behind me talking about Willow Creek Church. They began their conversation by talking about how large Willow is. I was not eavesdropping, but I could not help but hear them as they continued their evaluation of the church ... and of the pastor! I have to admit that I was quite interested to hear what else they had to say.

Having no idea that the teaching pastor of the church was sitting right in front of them, they continued on in their conversation. One of them asked, "What's the priest like in this church?" My ears really perked up as the other guy gave his take on things, "I hear he's like some of those TV evangelists; he *sweats* and *shouts* and *beats the sheep for money.*"

I was offended! I thought to myself, *I don't sweat that much!* The truth is, I am not a shouting preacher and I have never beat anyone in my church. These people had me tried, convicted, and executed, and they knew nothing about me!

I was pretty sure neither of these gentlemen had ever met me, and I was confident that I had never had a conversation with either of them. My suspicion was that neither of them had even attended a worship service at Willow Creek Church. It felt to me that someone had helped them form a hasty and hopefully inaccurate picture of me and the church, and it did not feel good.

Making the Connection

1. Tell about a time when you were judged wrongly and how you felt when this happened.

Knowing and Being Known

Read Matthew 7:1 – 5

2. What specific guidelines does Jesus give us when we are going to judge another person?

How might one of these guidelines impact the way you judge another person?

3. Jesus uses a vivid illustration to call us to serious self-evaluation before we judge others. What is the primary point of this illustration?

How might following Jesus' teaching in this illustration transform your life?

To Judge or Not to Judge

What does Jesus mean when he says, "Do not judge"? Does he mean we should never seek to discern anything about anyone else's words or deeds? Is he saying we should never make any assessments about anyone's attitude or conduct? Is he saying we can never try to determine if we're being set up or deceived by somebody? Does he mean for us to suspend all critical analysis, to downplay our discernment capabilities, to disregard the intuitive signals that come from the Holy Spirit? That can't be what Jesus is prohibiting! Jesus himself said, "I am sending you out like sheep among wolves. Therefore be as shrewd as snakes and as innocent as doves" (Matthew 10:16).

Jesus wants our critical capabilities to be at work. He expects us to be highly discerning people. He has given us minds to use and spiritual insight to identify wrong, evil, and danger. If this is all true, then what does Jesus mean when he says, "Do not judge"?

If you look at the whole of Scripture, it becomes obvious that what Jesus is prohibiting is vigilante justice — hasty, hostile, simplistic, and unmerciful interpersonal judgments. He is speaking against condemnations made without due process and executions carried out without a single question being asked. This kind of behavior undermines love. It destroys community. It creates inner personal defensiveness and distrust. And it violates the kingdom values of mercy and grace.

Read Matthew 7:1 – 2

4. In light of what you read in this passage and what you know from life experience, what are some of the possible consequences if we continue to pass harsh and ungodly judgment on others?

   • What consequences might we experience from those we judge?

THE PRINCIPLES OF JESUS

• What consequences might we face from those who observe our judgmental spirit?

• What consequences could we experience from God?

5. What is one example of good, healthy, Christ-honoring judgment?

How Would I Want Others to Judge Me?

The first step in learning to judge rightly is to ask the question, "How would I want others to judge me?" Jesus is clear that what goes around comes around. If we judge people harshly and without any mercy, we had better get ready to receive the same kind of judgment from them.

There are three important nuances when it comes to this process of judgment: First, ask yourself how you feel when others make hasty judgments about you. Reflect honestly on the pain this brings you and the injustice you feel. This will impact how you judge others.

Second, get to know others thoroughly before making judgments. Trying to judge others in a relational vacuum is always risky business.

Third, when you do feel led to judge another person, do it with a merciful heart. Remember the amazing grace and mercy God has extended to us and approach others with the same spirit.

If we come with these attitudes in our heart and mind, we will be able to extend righteous judgment that can lead to restoration and healing.

6. Why is relational connectedness so essential if we are going to judge others in a way that is redemptive and healing?

7. Why is remembering God's grace and mercy in one's life critical for those who want to judge in a righteous manner?

Stop and Look Closely at Your Own Sins

If we are going to judge others in a way that is pleasing to God, we should be profoundly aware of our human propensity to be far more critical of others than we are of ourselves.

Jesus says that whenever we are tempted to get the tweezers out so we can fix someone else's little problem, we had better learn to stop first and take some time for self-evaluation. Have you ever said, done, or thought of doing the exact same thing as the person you are about to pounce on? Through this kind of humble and honest self-evaluation we will begin to gain new perspective on how to interact with those we are about to judge.

Read Matthew 7:3 – 5

8. Respond to *one* of these statements:

☐ We tend to be most judgmental toward people who are most like us!

☐ It is easiest to see sins in others that are also sins we struggle to overcome in our own lives.

☐ If you struggle in an area of sin, you never have the right to judge someone else and point out sin in their life.

☐ If you truly love someone, you will look the other way and not point out their frailties, struggles, and sins!

9. Why is it essential to deal with sin in our own lives before God can use us to help another person face sin in their life?

10. What is one area of sin in your life that you feel God is calling you to face so that you can be a more effective servant for him?

How can your Christian friends pray for you and keep you accountable as you seek to face this area of sin and allow God to do spiritual eye surgery in your life?

Celebrating and Being Celebrated

As you close your study, offer up prayers of thanksgiving and celebration for God's amazing grace in your life. He is the One who knows you through and through, who sees all of your sin. He is the One who could judge and condemn you forever. Yet in his mercy he sent Jesus Christ to extend radical forgiveness. Give God praise for forgiving you when he could have judged you.

Loving and Being Loved

One of the hardest things we can do is admit we were wrong. Sadly, we have all had times we have wrongly judged another person and hurt them deeply in the process. Take time this week to think back over the past year. Has there been a time when you judged someone wrongly and hurt them by your attitude, words, or actions? If so, call the person this week or write him or her a note apologizing for your wrong judgment and asking for forgiveness.

Serving and Being Served

Make a commitment in your heart and with those you love to extend loving, biblical, grace-filled judgment to each other. Agree that you will seek to serve each other by never looking the other way when you see sin in each other's lives. Commit to going through a process of self-examination so that you will have clear eyes that can tenderly see sin in the lives of those you love and help them face and overcome that sin in the power of Jesus.

God's Inclination

MATTHEW 7:7 – 11

MANY STORIES AND LIFE SITUATIONS CONTAIN A PLOT AND A SUBPLOT. THE plot is the story that is plain to see, and the subplot is the hidden meaning just under the surface. This is the case in one of the most famous sets of books ever written, The Chronicles of Narnia. On the surface, it is a series of stories about a magical land with talking animals, a lion king named Aslan, Aslan's enemy—the wicked White Witch, and four children who end up visiting this enchanted land and having some amazing adventures.

But if you read the Chronicles of Narnia too quickly and fail to look at the story inside the story, you will miss many wonderful lessons that lie just under the surface. These children's stories tell about the love of God and salvation that is found in his only Son Jesus Christ. The stories unfold God's plan to overcome evil and to bring his children to a wonderful heavenly home!

We can read the Sermon on the Mount in a similar context. The lessons and the teachings of Jesus are the plot, the story on the surface, but if we slow down and look closely, we begin to see another story, a subplot that teaches us a great deal about Jesus, God the Father, and even ourselves.

We need to remember that there were two groups of people listening to Jesus that day. One group was celebrating the new truth they were hearing. This group was feeling joy, excitement, and anticipation for what was coming next. However, on that same mountainside there was another group of people who were not impressed by what they were hearing; they were angry. This group included the scribes, Pharisees, elders, and teachers of the Law. If we look beneath the surface of the Sermon on the Mount, we quickly see another drama unfolding. These religious leaders were so upset that they were beginning to plot the death of this rebel teacher!

Making the Connection

1. Tell about a story, book, or movie you have enjoyed that had a plot and a subplot.

Why is an understanding of the subplot needed to get the full impact of the story?

Knowing and Being Known

Read Matthew 7:7 – 11

Our God Is an Approachable Father

The Plot: Jesus wanted the people in the crowd that day to know that God is a heavenly Father who is very approachable! If you ever need anything from him, just ask. If you want to find him, just seek. If you're desperate, knock on the doors of heaven. He won't mind. He'd love to hear from you. He wants to know your concerns. There's no red tape, no drills, no hoops, no appointment secretaries to mess with. This announcement of a wide-open door to the Creator of the universe was wonderful news for many of the people in the crowd.

The Subplot: Although many in the crowd were overjoyed at the news that God is accessible, a part of the crowd was deeply troubled by what Jesus was teaching. For hundreds of years people had been taught that they could not have direct access to God. According to the laws of the old covenant, no average person on the street could come into the presence of God. The average person had to go to a local priest, the priest went to a high priest, and only the high priest himself could go into the presence of God, the Holy of Holies — and that was only once a year for a brief period of time. While these listeners were steeped in the outward observance (or technical aspects) of the law, they failed to see the heart of it. But now, on a mountainside in Galilee, Jesus was inviting everyone to walk freely into the office of the CEO of the universe. No local priest or high priest required, no hoops, no rituals, no sacrifices. Jesus is saying, "Walk right in." You better believe this caused a stir!

141

Read Matthew 7:7

2. What are the three word pictures Jesus uses to help us see that God is an approachable Father?

Why do you think Jesus used such common and ordinary examples?

3. What are the three promises contained in this verse?

How have you experienced the fulfillment of one of these promises in your life?

4. Jesus assures us that God is an accessible and inviting heavenly Father, yet sometimes we avoid coming to him. What are some of the things that keep us from coming to God with confidence that he will receive us warmly?

Our God Is a Benevolent Father

The Plot: Jesus taught the crowds that God is an enthusiastically benevolent Father. He loves to give people what they ask for; he longs to arrange for people to find what they are seeking; and he rejoices to open doors so that those on the outside of the kingdom can come in. God loves to surprise us with his goodness and ambush us with his grace. Once again, most people in the crowd accepted this teaching at face value and were excited to hear this wonderful news!

The Subplot: The tension was mounting! While many were excited to hear these words of Jesus, there were others who did not like what he was saying. All this talk of a benevolent and generous Father sounded borderline heretical to the traditionalists. For hundreds of years their priests had stressed legalistic activities to such an extent that God's true nature had become obscured by the constant demand for higher and higher levels of religious performance. Now Jesus was questioning their whole legalistic lifestyle. He was telling the crowd that God wanted to lavish them with his goodness without them doing a thing to earn it. Unheard of! There is no question that some of the people in the crowd were outraged by these claims of Jesus.

Read Matthew 7:8

5. Imagine yourself on the mountainside listening to Jesus that day. You have worked hard at keeping all the religious laws, but you feel as though you have failed miserably. How do you think you would feel as Jesus spoke these words?

6. What is one area of your life in which you have stopped asking, seeking, and knocking? Why have you stopped seeking God in this area?

7. In what area do you feel God wants you to begin asking, seeking, and knocking? How can your Christian friends encourage and support you as you begin seeking the Lord in this area?

Our God Is a Wise and Good Father

The Plot: Jesus taught the crowd that even though God is the omnipotent Creator of the universe, they could approach him as a wise and good Father. Jesus points out that most earthly fathers would not torment their children or tease them. The truth is, most earthly fathers try to love their children and give them good gifts. If imperfect fathers can show goodness and care, then how much more will our perfect heavenly Father extend goodness to his children! This was great news for many who heard Jesus teach. The idea of seeing God as a powerful but tender dad must have warmed their hearts.

The Subplot: This very well could have been the straw that broke the proverbial camel's back. The traditionalists were uncomfortable with the talk of God being approachable. They were irritated with all the talk of God being so benevolent. But now Jesus had crossed the line! He was telling the crowd that they could think of God as a good, wise dad. It was that "D" word that made some of the listeners go on ultimate tilt. You see, the religious traditionalists in the crowd were obsessively meticulous in how they addressed God. Jews were so worried they would profane the name of God that most wouldn't say or even spell the formal Hebrew word for God, *Yahweh*. In their minds, God was so holy that he needed to be kept at a safe distance. Now Jesus was inviting everyone on the mountainside to call Yahweh Daddy! It was just too intimate, too familiar; it lacked the reverence the traditionalists demanded. In their minds, this kind of talk was blasphemous. I believe that some of the people along the seashore that day began plotting a way to silence this Jesus, even if it meant they would have to kill him.

Read Matthew 7:9 – 11

8. What comparison is Jesus drawing between an earthly father and our heavenly Father?

9. What is one of the kindest things your earthly father has done for you? What is one of the kindest and most loving things your heavenly Father has done for you?

10. Tell about a biblical truth or life experience that has helped you receive and live in the truth that God is your heavenly Father.

Celebrating and Being Celebrated

Once a year we celebrate Father's Day. Yet we should celebrate the blessings we have received from our heavenly Father on a daily basis. Close your study with a time for praise, thanksgiving, and celebration of God as your Father. Consider using some of the suggestions below to direct this prayer time:

- Dear God, you are my heavenly Father and I thank you for all you provide for me. Thank you for ...
- Abba, Father, thank you that you are approachable. Thank you that you never close the door. I give you praise for ...
- God, you are my Daddy! I can look to you for protection in a pretty rocky world. I know I can trust you to watch over me because ...

Loving and Being Loved

Write a Father's Day card to your heavenly Father this week. Also, if you feel you have received love from your heavenly Father through the care, provision, and protection of your earthly father, write him a note as well, thanking him for letting God work through his life.

Serving and Being Served

As children, our parents serve us in countless ways. As adults, we have opportunity to serve them back. Take time this week to offer some practical act of service for your parents. Let them know you are thankful for all the ways they have served you over the years. If your parents are no longer living, consider some way you can serve them by doing something that will honor their name and memory.

THE
PARABLES
of JESUS

John Ortberg

Overcoming Growth Barriers

MATTHEW 13:3 – 23

I REMEMBER WHEN WE BROUGHT LAURA, OUR FIRST CHILD, HOME FROM THE hospital. I was struck by the rapid rate of her growth. At the hospital she weighed only about six pounds. She was a tiny thing! But she ate and ate and ate in unbelievable quantities. Over the first year of her life she gained twelve pounds and basically tripled her weight. Even when I found out that this growth rate is pretty common for babies, I was still amazed!

I was so impressed by this rapid growth, in fact, that I sat down and figured out what would happen if she continued on this growth curve every year. Believe it or not, our little baby girl would have weighed 486 pounds by the time she turned four!

I remember visiting friends of ours who had a nine-month-old baby. They were waiting with excitement and anticipation for the little guy to learn how to walk. Now, when you think about it, walking is a pretty common thing. Billions of people do it every day. Yet when it happened to their child, this mom and dad were cheering like it was the first time in the history of the world that anyone had walked. To them it was a miracle. They smiled, laughed, and coaxed him along. This was big stuff!

Making the Connection

1. Describe a time when you saw positive growth or development in some area of your life.

Knowing and Being Known

Read Matthew 13:3 – 9

2. In this parable, the sower and the seed are constant; they don't change. The variable in this story is the soil. Describe the four kinds of soil in this parable and what happened to the seed that fell on each kind of soil.

Failure to Thrive

There is actually a medical designation for babies who are not growing and developing as they should be. Doctors will write on a chart "FTT," which means "failure to thrive." Thriving is the natural condition of human beings. It is what a life is created by God to do. When there is a failure to thrive, doctors seek to identify the barrier to growth and remove it so that life will begin to thrive once more.

This is also very true in the spiritual realm. God has made us to grow, to thrive, to flourish spiritually. God wants us to love someone tomorrow whom we could not love yesterday. God wants sin to have less and less control of us as the years go by. God longs that we would share our faith more and more freely and with greater boldness and effectiveness simply because it is so central to our lives. He wants us to pray more deeply, speak more truthfully, rejoice more fully, and forgive more freely with every passing year. When we come to the end of our life, God wants people to say, "That person walked with God."

Read Matthew 13:18 – 23

3. What are some of the barriers Jesus identifies in this parable that can cause a person to "fail to thrive"?

The Problem of Hard-Heartedness

Jesus said some seed fell along the path. In the Israel of Jesus' day, hard-packed paths often ran near fields. Farmers and animals would walk on these paths. If seed fell on this kind of a hard surface, there was no chance it would grow. Jesus was saying that growth requires soil that is soft. If we replace the word *soil* with *heart*, we begin to understand the message Jesus was trying to convey.

Jesus understands that there are many people who have become hard-hearted toward God. These people have been disappointed, stepped on, and hurt a lot in life. They have become cynical and bitter and have allowed a protective coat to form around their heart so that God's seeds cannot penetrate. At this time, the evil one comes and snatches the seed away.

Knowing the meaning behind this parable should move us to do a "soil analysis" of our own heart. We need to be honest about whether our heart is hard, and do all we can to grow soft toward God.

Read Matthew 13:10 – 17

4. Jesus draws from the teaching of Isaiah as he portrays the condition of the human heart. How do you feel when you hear what Jesus says about the heart condition of human beings?

5. What is one life experience or lesson that has helped to soften your heart toward the things of God?

The Problem of Shallow Soil

The farmland of Jesus' day was rocky and shallow with only a few inches of topsoil. In many places, when roots would begin to spread and look for nutrition, all they would find was rock. Jesus wants us to know that growth requires soil that is soft and deep.

As we begin to do a soil analysis in our lives we may want to ask, "Is my faith putting down deep roots?" In his book *Celebration of Discipline*, Richard Foster writes, "Superficiality is the curse of this age." We live in a world of shallow relationships, superficial conversations, hurried moments of prayer, too much television, and light commitments.

This kind of shallowness has also invaded the church. We have all met people who go to church and have every appearance of a real love and devotion for God, but have no depth. Bouncing from one spiritual activity to another with great enthusiasm may make it seem like we are grabbing onto everything in the spiritual life with great gusto; however, at the end of the day, there are no deep roots.

6. Most cars have warning lights that come on to let us know when something is about to break down or overheat. What are some of the warning lights that go off in your heart when the roots of your faith are not going down deep into the things of God?

If you did a root analysis on your own life right now, where would you put yourself on the graph below?

0	1	2	3	4	5	6	7	8	9	10

My roots have no depth.

My roots are in the soil of God's presence, but need to be much deeper.

My roots are deep in the things of God.

7. What is one exercise, activity, or discipline that you have practiced to help till the soil of your heart, to slow you down, and to allow your roots to go deeper into the things of God?

The Problem of Weeds and Thorns

Some soil is deep enough and soft enough, but it is just too cluttered for anything to grow. The soil is wasting its valuable nutrients on weeds! The seed is being choked out by the competition. Clutter sounds like such a small problem, but I would suggest that this is possibly the most dangerous soil condition of all. It is dangerous because it is so subtle.

Jesus talked a lot about the clutter and lure of wealth. We live in a world where we are bombarded with promises that the accumulation of things will make us happy. I once saw an advertisement for a car that went something like this, "You can't buy happiness . . . but now you can lease it!" There is a magazine called *The Good Life*. If you read all of the advertisements in this magazine you'd get the sense that the good life consists primarily of two things: fine dining and weight reduction. Talk about a formula that will lead to clutter in your life! You can eat too much, get in a car and drive too fast to a health club that costs too much, and then get on a bike that goes nowhere!

8. Take a moment to do a personal clutter assessment. What are a few of the things (they don't have to be bad things) that seem to be the weeds and thorns that fill the garden of your life?

THE PARABLES OF JESUS

9. If you were going to do some weeding in your life, what is one easy and obvious weed you would need to pull?

What is one weed that might be a little tougher to pull, but still needs to go? How can your Christian friends pray for you and keep you accountable as you do this weeding project in your life?

We Are the Seed and the Sowers

While God is working in our lives, part of our growth is learning that we are not only the soil, but we are also called to be the sowers. Followers of Jesus Christ discover that they are called to scatter the seed of the good news of Jesus Christ freely and generously. We need to sow the seed everywhere we go, because we never know what soil is prepared and ready.

Many of us have worked, prayed, loved, and scattered seed faithfully, yet we have not seen the harvest we would have wanted. We have reached out to family or friends and invited them to church or shared our testimony or even had a chance to tell them the story of God's love given in Jesus Christ. But, as far as we can tell, nothing seems to be happening. In time, a part of us starts to think that either we did something wrong or that God is not keeping up his part of the deal.

This parable reminds us that not all soil is ready to receive God's seed. The sower can spread the seed freely, and the seed is ready to do its work, but not all of the soil is soft, deep, or free of weeds. Jesus wants us to remember that our part is only to sow the seed. Our job is not to make growth happen; only God can do that. We don't have to understand how it all works; we just need to sow the seed and let God do his work.

10. What is one way you have discovered that is natural for you to scatter seed and spread the message of Jesus Christ? (Consider ways your family or small group might work together to scatter seed and let others know that God loves them.)

Celebrating and Being Celebrated

There are times in all of our lives when we need to be honest and confess that our hearts have grown hard. If you are at that point, give God a little opening by offering the following humble and honest prayer of confession: "God, whatever you need to do, I want you to plow up the hardness of my heart. Please do it! I want to be tenderhearted toward you, but I can't do it on my own. Come and break up the hard soil of my life." Then thank God for hearing your prayer and be prepared for him to answer it.

Loving and Being Loved

One of the greatest acts of love we could ever express is to freely scatter the seed of the good news of Jesus Christ. This saving message and the love of God can change lives forever. Identify one person in your life who has not yet received the grace of God through Jesus Christ. Commit yourself to pray for that person daily over the coming month. Pray for the soil of his or her heart to grow soft and receptive to the seed of the gospel (the message and person of Jesus). Also, ask God to show you creative and effective ways to scatter the seed of the gospel in this person's life.

Serving and Being Served

Sometimes God uses us to help till the soil of a hard-hearted person. Identify a person in your life who seems very hard to the things of God. Commit to extend one act of service to this person in the coming week. Bathe this action in prayer and ask God to use it as part of his process of softening the person's heart.

Overcoming Resentment

MATTHEW 20:1 – 16

WE LIVE IN A WORLD OF INSIDERS AND OUTSIDERS, THOSE WHO HAVE AND those who have not. Children learn at a young age what it means to be in a club or the gut-wrenching feeling of knowing you are not welcome. When a young girl tries out for a sports team and makes it, she knows the exhilaration of being "on the team." And when a young man runs for student council but does not get elected, he knows the deep pain of being on the outside. This continues on into adulthood in the marketplace and in social settings.

What is true today was also true two thousand years ago in Jesus' day. In the first century, the vineyard was a common metaphor for the people of Israel. Throughout the Old Testament, this image was used to help God's people understand many lessons about themselves. Consider this example from Isaiah 5:1, 7:

> I will sing for the one I love
> a song about his vineyard:
> My loved one had a vineyard
> on a fertile hillside ...
> The vineyard of the LORD Almighty
> is the nation of Israel,
> and the people of Judah
> are the vines he delighted in.

The parable we are going to study in this session may sound as if it is about a vineyard, but what it is really about is the family of God—about who is inside the family of God and who is outside. It is a parable that gives us a window into the heart of God, who wants everyone to know that they are invited to be on the inside of his family.

In a world of fences and membership cards there should be one place where the doors are wide open—the church! And there should be one family that is never a closed circle—the family of God. Jesus threw the doors wide open and made access possible for all of us! No place in all the earth should be more inviting and welcoming than the church of Jesus Christ, and no one should have wider arms than a Christian.

Making the Connection

1. Describe a time when you made the team, were invited in, or found yourself on the inside of a closed circle. If you can't think of an example, then describe a time when you did not make the cut, were excluded, or found yourself clearly on the outside of a closed circle. How did you feel?

Knowing and Being Known

Read Matthew 20:1 – 16

2. What is unusual about the landowner's hiring practices and compensation program in this parable?

How do the landowner's practices reflect the way God reaches out to lost people and invites them into his family?

3. In this parable five groups of workers are hired and eventually paid. How do you feel the last group of workers (who had only worked one hour) felt about their compensation in relationship to how the first group of workers (who had worked for twelve hours) felt about their pay for the day of work?

The Poison of Performance-Based Christianity

The workers hired at the first hour of the day represent those in the church who operate on a performance-based approach to life and faith. This can happen to some who have spent a lifetime in the church (the vineyard). Because these people have avoided certain scandalous sins, they begin to feel that God is getting a pretty good deal with them. Instead of rejoicing at those who come in at the last minute, they can begin to have a grumbling, resentful, judgmental spirit.

Then there are those who have what we could call grace-based Christianity. These are the latecomers, those who have no contract and no guarantees. They are desperate, in need of anything and everything Jesus can offer them. Their whole relationship with God is based on trust. These people are seized by joy over their good fortune. They are humbled because God is so good to them. They marvel at the greatness of God's character and are motivated to work in the vineyard out of profound gratitude to him.

4. How can performance-based Christianity poison the heart of the person who is caught up in it?

How can performance-based Christianity poison the health and witness of a local church?

5. When a person is captured by grace-based Christianity and over-whelmed by God's goodness, how is this reflected in his or her daily life?

A Complaining Spirit

Sometimes those who have been in the church for a long time can adopt a joyless spirit. When this poison begins to run through their veins, they become joy-challenged. These people actually seek out other complainers in order to justify their sinful disposition. They become blind to the good things around them and, if they do happen to notice anything good, they fail to celebrate or praise those things. Instead, they obsess over bad things and want everyone else to see them and obsess with them. This kind of complaining, joyless spirit is deadly and can kill both a church and the heart of a follower of Christ.

The antidote to a complaining spirit is the discipline of noticing. We need to learn how to pay attention, to slow down, and see what God has done and is doing all around us. Then we need to declare and celebrate where God is at work.

6. The workers who had put in a full day and got a full denarius (exactly what they were promised) grumbled and complained (verse 11). When you look at the story from where they stood, how might you sympathize with their frustration and complaining?

How have you seen a grumbling spirit hurt the health and life of a church?

7. The antidote to a complaining and grumbling spirit is developing a thankful spirit through slowing down and noticing all of God's goodness. What can you do to slow down the pace of your life over the coming month so you can make space for thankfulness?

A Resentful Spirit

Another mark of performance-based Christianity is a resentful spirit. This occurs when we experience God as a strict taskmaster and not as a loving Father. Resentment grows when we feel we always have to do something to gain God's love and approval. Instead of feeling like a deeply loved child, we feel like a dutiful soldier or loyal servant. It becomes harder and harder to believe that God really loves us just for who we are. Even if we immerse ourselves in all sorts of activities and commitments as Christians, a resentful spirit keeps us from drinking deeply at the fountain of Christ and experiencing restoration for our soul.

The antidote for a resentful spirit is to receive God's love for us. We need to reflect deeply on all God has done to show his love. Resentment begins to die when our hearts are gripped by the overwhelming reality of God's love for us.

8. How did the resentful spirit of the first group of workers in this parable (verse 12) impact the way they saw the other workers? How can this same negative attitude infect the church today and keep us from reaching those outside the family of God?

9. Read 1 John 3:1–3 and 4:9–10. How can a deep and clear understanding of God's love for us help us overcome performance-based Christianity?

A Judgmental Spirit

The first group of workers in this parable were deeply upset because the landowner had treated those who came to work in the final hour of the day as equal with them. The laborers who put in a full day's work expressed their displeasure with these telling words, "You have made them equal to us" (verse 12). There is a judgmental spirit here. "I have worked so hard and they slip in under the wire and get all the blessing I deserve! Where is the fairness in that? I am sacrificing more. I am suffering more. I'm the one doing all the work."

The antidote to this kind of a spirit is remembering. We need to remember that we are all latecomers! None of us can sit in a place of judgment because we have all come into God's family (his vineyard) by grace. We also need to remember that God dispenses gifts, not wages. Even those who work all day receive only a gift. None of us gets paid according to merit — if we did, we would all end up in hell! How incredible it is to remember that, instead of punishment, God has shown us his great mercy and lavished us with his goodness.

10. Describe a time when you were amazed and overwhelmed with a deep personal sense of God's love and affection for you.

11. If you came into the family of God at a young age, how is this fact a reminder of God's grace in your life and his provision for you? Or, if you came into the family of God late in life, how have you experienced God's grace through his open invitation?

Celebrating and Being Celebrated

Every day we are lavished with gifts of grace. Each breath of life, each morning we wake up, each smile someone gives, each greeting and word of encouragement are reminders of God's grace. When we see a flower blossoming in spring, when we pick up a Bible and feed on the Word of God, when we walk into church to the sound of worship music, we are receiving grace! Yet even though we are surrounded by the goodness of God, we oftentimes don't even notice it. We need to develop eyes that see, a heart that responds, and lips that give praise to God. Take a few moments to consider three or four gifts or blessings God has lavished on you today, and then offer a prayer of thanksgiving to him.

Loving and Being Loved

If you are going to effectively communicate the love of Jesus to others, you need to receive his love fully. Take fifteen minutes three or four times in the coming week and find a quiet place where you can sit down and meditate deeply on 1 John 3:1–3:

> See what great love the Father has lavished on us, that we should be called children of God! And that is what we are! The reason the world does not know us is that it did not know him. Dear friends, now we are children of God, and what we will be has not yet been made known. But we know that when Christ appears, we shall be like him, for we shall see him as he is. All who have this hope in him purify themselves, just as he is pure.

Memorize this passage and let the truth of God's love sink deeply into your heart. As you memorize the passage, personalize it. Know that it is telling you who you are and how much the Father loves you. Ask God to overwhelm you with the height and depth and breadth of his love. Remember that spiritual giants are ordinary people who have come to understand that they are dearly loved by the Father. Pray that your understanding of God's love will overflow to others.

Serving and Being Served

The greatest act of service we could ever offer to another person is to clearly communicate the love of God and the grace of Jesus Christ. List a few people you know who are not yet followers of Christ:

Pray for each of these people each day using the following cues to direct your prayer time:

- Pray that your life would be so filled with love, joy, and grace that your friends will see Christ alive and at work in you.
- Pray that your church (all the people of God in your congregation) will have a growing heart to reach out to those who are not yet followers of Jesus Christ.
- Pray for your heart to be cleansed of any complaining, resentment, or judgmental attitude so that you are a clean vessel through which God can work.
- Pray that God will give you an opportunity to tell your story of faith or to talk about the good news of God's love in Jesus Christ with each of the people on your prayer impact list.

Don't Wait Until It's Too Late

MATTHEW 25:1 – 13

HAVE YOU EVER HAD A DREAM LIKE THIS? YOU SHOW UP AT SCHOOL FOR A class you have been taking all semester long. As you walk into the room you suddenly realize that it is the day of a big test, but you forgot about it. You did not study and are hopelessly unprepared. You sit there and know you don't have a chance of passing.

There is a story about a college student who has an experience like this. He is taking a class on ornithology (the study of birds). It is a very difficult class and the professor is famous for being a pretty tough character. The student thinks he is prepared, but with this professor, you never really know.

The day of the class final, the student walks in only to find no blue books or exam papers. Instead, there are twenty-five photographs of birds' feet hanging on the walls. The professor explains that the entire final exam is to identify the species of each bird by recognizing their feet.

This student is in shock. He is outraged as he realizes he does not have a chance of passing this test. Finally, he speaks up. "This is too hard. I studied. I tried to prepare. But no one can pass a test like this!"

The professor responds, "Too bad, that's the final."

The student shoots back, "This is completely unfair and I refuse to take the final."

The professor then informs the student (and the entire class) in no uncertain terms, "You will take this final or I will fail you right now!"

The student says, "Then fail me!"

The professor says, "Young man, what is your name? You just flunked Ornithology 101!"

At which the young man looks at the professor, takes off his shoes, and says, "You tell me!"

Whether this story actually took place is not the point. It is a humorous but clear reminder that when you are a student it is wise to remember that the final always comes. The wise student does not wait until the last minute and then cram for the exam. Likewise, in life, our final moment might not be today or tomorrow, but it is coming. Never doubt it. If we are wise, we will live as those who are ready.

Making the Connection

1. Describe a dream or fear you have experienced about being late or unprepared. Or, tell about a time when you thought you could wait "a little bit longer" and got caught unprepared.

Knowing and Being Known

Read Matthew 25:1–13

2. How were the two groups of virgins in this story similar and how were they different?

What consequences did the second group of virgins face because of this one difference?

THE PARABLES OF JESUS

3. If you had to give this parable a title that gets to the heart of the message Jesus is communicating, what would it be?

No-Regret Finances

How many of us have made a financial choice that we later regretted? The truth is, most of us have! Yet Jesus would have us look at finances from an eternal perspective. He wants us to ask, "How will this investment look to me the day I die?" Most investment counselors don't think about the scope of eternity. But we need to.

Due to the affluence of our society, we have many choices regarding how to spend our money. We need to strive to live in such a way that when we look back we won't have to say, "If only I had it to do over again, I would have invested so much more in the things that really matter!"

Read 2 Corinthians 9:6 – 11

4. The apostle Paul gives a vision for how a follower of Christ approaches finances. Describe how God wants to impact our *attitude* and our *actions* when it comes to sharing what we have.

5. How might a spiritual skeptic view a follower of Christ who takes this call to generosity seriously?

6. Take a moment to plot where you see yourself on the two graphs below:

0	1	2	3	4	5	6	7	8	9	10

I give very
sparingly.

I give some of what God
has given me.

I am intentionally
generous in my giving.

0	1	2	3	4	5	6	7	8	9	10

I give because I
feel pressure but
don't find joy in it.

I give and find some
satisfaction in
supporting God's work.

I find deep joy in giving
and do it cheerfully.

What needs to happen in your life for you to take the next step in your giving and become more generous toward God and his work?

If you have had experiences when giving was joy-filled, describe what helped you grow as a cheerful giver.

No Regret When It Comes to Sin

Have you ever seen bad habits simply go away? You used to chew your nails, or call other drivers bad names, or lose your temper all the time. Then one day these behaviors simply disappear. You wake up and they are gone.

Of course not! That is just not the way bad habits work, and even less the way that sin works. Think back to the story of Cain in the Bible. Cain wanted to serve God, but his soul was poisoned with envy toward his brother. God said to Cain, "If you do what is right, will you not be accepted? But if you do not do what is right, sin is crouching at your door; it desires to have you, but you must rule over it" (Genesis 4:7).

Some of us need to identify the truth that sin is crouching at our door and that its desire is for us. If we simply quiet our hearts and ask God to show us, we will see danger areas such as bad habits, destructive patterns, abuse, addiction, racism, pride, judgment, chronic deceit, gossiping, dishonesty, sexual misbehavior, sharp-tongued sarcasm, attitudes that wither our spirit, and a host of other sins.

But we need not fall victim to the sins that lie in wait for us. We are not passive victims who have no way of escape. If we are committed to mounting a full-scale attack, by God's grace we can master the sinful habits in our lives.

Read Genesis 4:6 – 16

7. What was God's warning to Cain about the temptation of sin, and how did Cain respond to this warning?

What are some of the ways God seeks to warn us about the potential consequences of our sins?

8. What were some of the consequences of Cain's decision to do things his way instead of God's way?

What is one consequence you have faced in your life because you decided to follow the enticement of sin and not the warnings of God?

9. One of the best deterrents to sin is honestly looking at what we might regret later. Choose *one* of the scenarios below and seek to list some of the possible consequences or regrets in the life of a person who chooses to follow the path of sin and not the counsel of God:

☐ A person in the workplace who is tempted to "borrow" supplies and small sums of money he or she feels no one will ever notice are gone

☐ A married person who is feeling enticed to pursue a friendship and one-on-one time with a person of the opposite sex toward whom he or she feels a strong attraction

☐ A person who has a growing need for alcohol to carry him or her through the day

No Regret When It Comes to Taking Risks

God calls all of his followers to be willing to take some risks for his sake. The nation of Israel is a classic example of a people who failed to take risks. God called the Israelites to go into the Promised Land and take it in his power. But even after having witnessed the Passover and God's mighty deliverance from Egypt through the parting of the Red Sea, the Israelites were not willing to put their trust in God. They were literally standing on the edge of God's promise and all they had to do was take a step and cross over, but they refused because of their fear. They would not take the risk. Many of them went to their graves never having stepped foot on the Promised Land.

Read Numbers 13:1 – 2, 26 – 33; 14:6 – 9

10. Twelve men went into the Promised Land to investigate what it was like. Describe the report and attitude of the ten who were opposed to entering the land, and also the attitude of the two who wanted to enter the land.

The negative report had significant impact on the whole nation of Israel. What regrets do you think the nation of Israel had about not taking the risk and entering the land?

11. What is one risk you feel God might want you to take that you have been resisting? How can your Christian friends pray for you and encourage you to step out in faith and take this risk?

Celebrating and Being Celebrated

One key to growing in generosity is recognizing all of the good things God has poured out on your life. When we see his generosity, we become freer to give. As you celebrate God's bottomless gift of generosity toward you, pray for the willingness to show that same generosity to others.

Loving and Being Loved

God has revealed his love for us by sending his Son to die on a cross and pay for our sins. He calls us to respond in love by repenting of sin and turning from ongoing sinful practices. In the coming days, show your love for God by identifying one area in your life in which you are facing ongoing temptation. Use the following process as you seek to express your love for God and walk in his ways:

1. Identify a very specific area in which you are facing temptation:

   _____

   _____

2. Confess this area of temptation to God and ask him to fill you with the power of his Holy Spirit to resist it.

3. Write down some of the very real and specific consequences you might face if you continue to walk in the way of sin and not follow the leading of God in this area:

4. Invite one close Christian friend to pray for you and keep you accountable to honor God in this area of your life.

Serving and Being Served

We are called to be cheerful givers. Consider a radical act of service in the coming month. Pray about one possession you have that you feel God might want you to give up. Sell this item and give the resources to your church or some mission organization. Be sure to pray for God to give you a joyous spirit in this adventure of giving. Let this be a first step in your life toward no-regret finances.

An Invitation to Return Home

LUKE 15:11 – 24

IN OUR LIVES, WE CHOOSE DAILY BETWEEN TWO ALTERNATIVES: WE EITHER choose to live at home with the Father or away in a distant land. When we are at home with the Father we invite God to be with us all day. We know that we can be in constant communication with him, so we ask him to get rid of any thoughts that don't please him. We know that our primary identity is that we are his beloved children, so we are not easily threatened or made anxious. We know that we are perfectly safe in his hands, so we are not easily discouraged by problems and challenges. God's deepest desire is for us to live at home with him and walk in this peace.

But there is another way to live. In the language of the passage we will study today it is "to be in a distant country." When we live in a distant country we don't often think of God. To be reminded of him just makes us feel guilty for some of the choices we have made. Sins like deceit or gossip become increasingly attractive. We no longer have an inner sense of freedom, but instead feel weighed down because we know something is wrong. When we are in this "distant country" we feel hurried, rushed, easily irritated, and often threatened. We search for bursts of pleasure but cannot find sustained joy.

Making the Connection

1. Describe how you have felt when you have been close to the Father and had your feet planted firmly at home.

   Describe how you have felt when you have wandered to a distant land.

Knowing and Being Known

Read Luke 15:11 – 24

2. What decisions did the son make and what attitudes did he display that led him to a pig's trough?

   What decisions did he make and what attitude changes occurred to lead him back to his father?

3. What do you learn about the heart and character of the father in this story?

Crossroad #1: Temptation

For the prodigal son, the temptation stage came before this story ever begins. Somewhere along the line a thought occurred to him, "Living at home is a burden. I would be happier away from my father and without all these constraints in my life."

We see this in kids sometimes. Some children are very compliant and love to be home with their parents. Others are not nearly as compliant and pose much more of a challenge.

James Dobson writes about a two-year-old named Frankie who was a noncompliant child. He tells how Frankie pulled a chair over to the front window and carefully placed it inside the drapes. He was standing there looking out at the world beyond his window when his mother came looking for him. She saw his little white legs protruding beneath the drapes and quietly slipped in behind him. Then she heard her two-year-old boy speaking to himself in very sober terms, "I gotta get out of here."

In this parable we meet a young man who is saying, "I gotta get out of here! Here at home I always have to do what my father says. I have to work in his fields, eat at his table, follow his rules. I don't want to have to do this anymore. My life would be better if I had no rules. I could be my own boss; I could chart my own course. I gotta get out of here!"

4. Describe a time when you faced temptation, considered the consequences, and said no. When you look back, why are you glad you made the right choice? What might it have cost you had you entered into this area of temptation?

5. Describe a time when you faced temptation and entered in. What do you wish you had done differently? Describe the cost you and others paid because of this decision to live outside the Father's will.

Crossroad #2: Action

This huge step moves us from considering and thinking about a temptation to pursuing a sinful course of action. For the prodigal son this step occurred when he went to his father and asked for his inheritance. He had convinced himself that he had a right to his father's property. In truth, the property rightfully belonged to his father, both legally and ethically.

If most people toy around with the idea of sin long enough, they will eventually move into action. Whatever the sin, the movement from thought to action always happens at the same point: when the person finds an acceptable ratio-nale or pretext to do it. Rationalizing is universal among fallen people. Some people say, "It's just a harmless conversation or flirtation," when they know an unhealthy attraction is grow-ing. Others rationalize by saying to themselves, "The company does not pay me enough, and I work a lot of extra hours," as they pad expense accounts and begin to steal from their employer. If you see yourself rationalizing a behavior, watch out! Are you about to take the giant step from temptation into action that James warns us about (James 1:14 – 16)?

6. When you have faced temptation in the past, what has helped you stand strong and resist it?

7. Describe the end results of the son's decisions and how these are like the end results of our actions when we choose to leave the Father.

8. Identify one area in your life in which you are standing at a crossroad that will take you from temptation to action. How can your Christian friends pray for you and challenge you to resist the temptation and not enter into this action that will take you away from the Father?

Crossroad #3: Pain

Some time ago I was about to have surgery on my knee. When I asked the doctor what I could expect after the surgery, he answered in one word, "Pain." He informed me that there would be two primary ways I could deal with the pain. The first way would be to take some pills that would not deal with the source of the problem but would mask the pain for a little while. The second way to deal with the pain would be to face it. He then warned me that the pills would last for only a short while and then I would have to begin rehabilitation and deliberately experience pain in order to build up my body and be well and whole again.

In my first rehab session after surgery I had one of the most sensitive and tender therapists I could imagine. Each time she asked me to make any movement she would ask if I was feeling pain. If I said yes or she thought I looked like I was experiencing any discomfort, she would stop. There was not much pain, *but there was also not much progress.*

For my next session I got a physical therapist with a radically different approach to therapy. She was a solid, strong woman who was ferociously committed to my long-term health and wellness. She had me lay on my stomach and then she grabbed the foot on my injured leg and bent it back as far as her heavily muscled arms could bend it. I said, "I'm feeling some pain." She responded with an enthusiastic, "Yes! Feel the pain! Embrace the pain! The pain is our friend!" It was a whole different session in terms of pain, *but we made amazing progress.*

9. In this parable the son finally hits the wall of pain (verses 14–16).
   Describe the son's response to his pain in *one* of the following areas:

   ☐ How he viewed himself

   ☐ How he viewed his father

   ☐ How he viewed his future

10. How has God used the crossroad of pain in your life to bring you back
    into his arms?

Crossroad #4: Living As a Child of God or a Hired Servant

Once the son hits the crossroad of pain, he has to make a decision. Will he continue to live in ever-increasing levels of pain away from the father or will he humble himself and go home? The pain wakes him up and he is finally ready to go back to his father. But as he prepares himself, he also reveals his own sense of unworthiness. He writes a little speech that he is ready to give to his father when he arrives home (verses 18–19). In this speech he reveals the fact that he no longer sees himself as a beloved son of the father, but worthy only of the status of a hired servant.

As a hired servant he will be a free man with his own income and will live in the village. He can keep a certain level of autonomy. He might be able to pay back to his father some of what he has squandered and may even be able to render helpful services. However, he will never again know the intimacy of a son with a father. He will never again feel the warmth and tenderness of knowing a father is looking on him with favor and joy.

But the father has a whole different plan in mind!

11. What contrast do you see between how the son sees himself and how the father sees him (verses 17–24)?

12. This parable reveals the heart of the Father toward you. How would you describe the disposition of God's heart toward you today?

Celebrating and Being Celebrated

Close your study with a time of prayer thanking God for treating you as a beloved daughter or son. Give him praise that he does not put you on probation as a hired servant, but that his arms and home are always open.

Loving and Being Loved

During the coming week, read and reflect deeply on Hebrews 12:4–13. Examine your own personal history and the times God has brought the loving pain of discipline to your life. Take time in prayer to thank him for loving you enough to discipline you.

Serving and Being Served

The truth of God's unyielding fatherly affection is life-changing. Commit to writing a note to one or two friends who are followers of Christ reminding them that they are beloved children of the Father. Communicate what you have learned from this study and let them know that you felt prompted to remind them of one of the greatest truths in the world—they are a beloved child of God.

Heart-Healing Forgiveness

LUKE 7:36 – 50

IN EVERY CULTURE VARIOUS KINDS OF ETIQUETTE SURROUND MANY ASPECTS of life. Mealtime etiquette is certainly one of these areas. In some cultures it is considered a compliment to belch after a meal; in other cultures this is seen as quite rude. For some people, elbows on the table can be seen as offensive. There are rules for setting a table, for who gets served first, for conversation, and for what to do after a meal. Consider a couple of the following situations. What do you think is the proper behavior based on rules of etiquette?

When should one start eating the main course at a formal dinner?
A. After the hostess is served
B. After the hostess lifts her fork
C. After three or four people are served
D. A.S.A.P. with urgency and passion

When should the hostess be served first?
A. Never
B. If it's her birthday
C. If the first portion is hard to extract
D. If she's a greedy pig

The answer to both of these questions according to Emily Post, an etiquette expert, is "C."

Rules of etiquette help govern how we behave in social settings. No one is thrown in jail for breaking these rules, but they can impact how people feel. Following them can affirm a person and breaking them can be very insulting.

Making the Connection

1. What are some commonly accepted rules of etiquette in our culture?

Tell a story about a time when you broke a rule of etiquette.

Knowing and Being Known

Read Luke 7:36 – 39, 40 – 47

Breaking All the Rules

In this passage, we need to notice the gross neglect that occurred when Jesus came to this home as a visiting rabbi. There was no kiss of greeting, no washing of the feet, no anointing with oil. These were not subtle omissions easily overlooked. Simon was breaking every rule of etiquette when it came to having an honored guest in his home. Jesus was ignored and insulted, and every indication is that it was quite deliberate — an intentional slap in the face. Every one of the guests would have felt the tension in the room.

Into this scene a woman enters. Luke gives us some very specific information about this woman: she was a sinner (verse 37). From the Greek word Luke uses, it is quite clear that she was a very specific kind of sinner, a prostitute. This is a woman who wouldn't have been invited to a dinner like this in a million years, yet she approaches the table. Jesus and the other guests would have been reclining at the table with their feet extended away from it. Now it is the woman's turn to break a whole different set of rules of etiquette.

Simon had not greeted Jesus with a kiss, but this woman lavishes Jesus with kisses on his feet. Jesus' feet were still dirty from the dusty streets as no one had offered to wash them when he entered the banquet. The woman begins to wash his feet with her tears and dry them with her hair. Simon had not offered oil for anointing when Jesus entered, but this sinful woman pours out all she has from the perfume flask she wore around her neck.

2. Imagine you were a guest at the table and you had watched Simon's conduct at this dinner. How might you have felt toward him?

How might you have felt toward the woman and her breaches of etiquette?

3. What does Simon's etiquette-breaking neglect teach you about the condition of his heart?

What do the woman's etiquette-breaking actions teach you about the condition of her heart?

4. Look at this parable as a mirror reflecting the condition of your heart. How do you see yourself reflected as you look at each of these rule breakers?

A Story of Two Debtors

In Jesus' day people called moneylenders would offer to help people out of a jam by loaning them money at very high interest rates. In those days, people who allowed themselves to get into debt were not highly thought of. And those who would lend out money at interest were seen as an even worse class of people. They were shady characters. In our day this story would begin, "Let me tell you about two bookies who were in over their heads to a loan shark called Big Louie."

In this story, both debtors owe money and neither of them can pay it back. Both men face the same fate. The only difference is that while one of the debts looks manageable and the debtor carries the illusion that maybe there is a way out, the other guy knows he is desperate. The truth is, both of these debtors could expect to lose all they had, with only prison or worse to look forward to. Just then the loan shark calls them in and says, "I'm going to make you an offer you can't refuse" — and promptly forgives both debts.

Jesus then asks Simon and the people at the table which of these two debtors was going to have his world turned upside down. Which one would be filled with relief, gratitude, and joy? Which would be seized by love for the one who forgave his debt? Jesus poses a very simple question to Simon, "Which of them will love him more?" Simon sees where this is headed, but all eyes are on him so he has to answer. He says, "I *suppose* the one who had the bigger debt." Jesus says — I think with a little humor — "You have judged correctly!"

5. In this story Jesus uses the two debtors to represent Simon the Pharisee and the sinful woman. As you look at this entire passage, what do these two people have in common and how are they different?

6. Jesus is deeply concerned about the sins of pride and self-righteousness. What are some of the warning signs that spiritual pride is growing in a person's heart and life?

7. Jesus longs for us to come to him in genuine humility, aware of our sin and need for his grace. What has helped you grow in humility and clarify your perspective in relationship to Jesus?

Everything Put in Perspective

Now the drama changes significantly. Up to this point Jesus has been interacting with Simon, but now Jesus turns toward the woman, who is on the ground behind him. This would mean that Jesus had to, in effect, turn his attention away from Simon and all the guests at the table. Jesus faces the woman, but as he does, he continues to talk to Simon.

He asks Simon if he has seen the woman. Well, of course he has — everyone has seen her. Yet Simon had seen only a theological object lesson or a focal point for his contempt. He had not seen what Jesus saw — no one had. At this moment Jesus makes a gracious but powerful series of declarations. He reminds Simon that he had not provided foot washing but that this woman had used her own tears to wash his feet and her own hair to dry them. Jesus points out Simon's failure to give a kiss of greeting, and celebrates this woman's lavish freedom with kissing his feet. Then Jesus reminds Simon, and everyone around the table, that he had not been offered oil for his head, but this woman had poured out precious perfume on his feet. Jesus announces to everyone gathered around the table, and to anyone else who is in earshot, that this woman is the one who has been forgiven much and who has loved much.

Now Simon has to figure out how he fits into the parable Jesus had told just minutes earlier. If this woman was the one who was forgiven much and who loved much, who was Simon?

Read Luke 7:44 – 50

8. Imagine yourself at the table as a guest at this banquet. Jesus, the visiting rabbi, has just spoken these powerful words to Simon, host of the banquet. As you look around the room, describe what you think is going through the mind of *one* of the following people:

   ☐ Simon

   ☐ The sinful woman

   ☐ Jesus

   ☐ You as one of the guests

9. Describe the last time you found yourself at the feet of Jesus in deep worship, amazed at his grace and celebrating his love.

10. What can you do in your schedule and personal disciplines to make more time to be at the feet of the Savior?

Celebrating and Being Celebrated

As you close in prayer, move in two very distinct directions. First, take time for confession. Confess sins of self-righteousness and pride. Confess any sense of feeling that you deserve God's grace on your own merit. Second, take time for humble adoration. Spend some moments at the feet of Jesus. You might even want to kneel as you pray.

Loving and Being Loved

In this story we meet a religious leader who has come to a place of exalting himself and looking down on others, especially sinners. He has forgotten that he is just as sinful as this woman and, in some ways, maybe more sinful. In his mind, she is an outsider, undesirable. Yet Jesus taught that all are welcome at his table if they come as ones who love and worship him.

This story raises the question: who is really the big debtor? Everyone could see that there was great sin at that banquet table, but it was not the sin that Simon assumed. It was the sin of lips that wouldn't kiss, knees that wouldn't kneel, eyes that wouldn't weep, and hands that wouldn't serve. It was the sin of perfume that would never leave the jar, the sin of a heart that would not break, a life that would not change, and a soul too stubborn and proud to love.

Take time in the coming weeks to ask the Holy Spirit to reveal any prejudice or pride in your life when it comes to who you believe is welcome in the church. Sometimes there are certain individuals or groups of people we would rather not see show up at our church or in our fellowship. If God brings to your heart anyone you have judged as unworthy of his grace and unwelcome among his people, commit yourself to praying for three things in the coming days:

1. Pray for a broken spirit and a humble heart so that you can see yourself as needing grace just as much as this person does.
2. Pray for the Lord to work in this person's heart and soften him or her toward the things God has to offer.
3. Pray for God to use you to extend love and grace to this person in some practical way in the coming week. In addition, pray for an opportunity to invite him or her to visit your church, or even to your home for a meal.

Serving and Being Served

Sometimes our service is rendered to those in need; at other times it is extended to those who are part of our church community. In this story, the service is being offered humbly to Jesus not by the religious leader, but by the sinful woman who takes what is most precious to her and pours it on Jesus' feet. During the coming week, reflect deeply on your own commitment to worship Jesus with all your heart. Are you giving him your best and laying it at his feet? Do you worship passionately, give generously, sing joyfully, and learn humbly? Over the coming month, seek to take deeper steps in serving Jesus by going deeper as his worshiper.

Spiritual Sincerity

MATTHEW 21:28 – 32

A STORY IN TWO ACTS.

In the first act we meet a family sitting around the breakfast table: a father, a mother, and two grown sons. Both boys work on the family farm. Dad tells son number one to go work the back forty. This first son is a bit surly and strong-willed. On top of that, he is not above mouthing off to Dad and being outright stubborn. He wears ripped jeans and a T-shirt and has a pack of cigarettes in his sleeve. He looks up from his Pop-Tart and says, "Me? The back forty? Long hours, minimum pay, backbreaking labor? I don't think so!" He gets up from the table and tells his dad, "It's not going to fit into my schedule today!" He walks out of the house, jumps on his Harley, and heads off to see his heavily-tattooed, body-pierced girlfriend.

The father turns toward his other son. This son is wearing khaki pants and a button-down oxford shirt and is eating a bowl full of Wheaties.

Have you ever noticed that when one child is misbehaving, another one will get so sweet? When the father gives the same command to this son, he is cheerful and compliant. He goes so far as to say, "I'll go, sir!" which is exactly what his father wants to hear. The second boy is the good boy, the helpful child, the shining light in his father's galaxy—at least for the moment.

This second son reminds me of a character from the old show *Leave It to Beaver*. Eddie Haskell was a friend of Wally Cleaver who was always giving compliments and buttering up every adult who crossed his path, but as soon as they were gone his true colors came out. This second son is a modern-day Eddie Haskell. He says, "The back forty? Sure, Dad! It would be an honor for me. Maybe there are some who don't appreciate such a great opportunity to work, but I would love to spend the day out there working for you. What a privilege to serve! As a matter of fact, just this morning, during my rather lengthy time of prayer and Scripture reading I was actually thinking how much I love to work in the back forty." You get the point. There is a phony willingness to his enthusiasm.

Dad and Mom look at their model son and think how proud they are to have such a willing, helpful, and cooperative child. He is the hero of the breakfast table. But remember, this is only the first act of the drama. There is more to come.

In the second act, the tough and resistant son gets on his Harley and begins driving, but something happens. He can't get his father's words out of his mind. As he is riding away he begins thinking of his father and all this man has done for him over the years. With time, his heart softens and he hits the brakes. He makes a U-turn on his Harley, heads back home, and drives out to the back forty. When he gets there he picks up his tools and starts to work. A moment later, his father comes around the corner. To his surprise, he sees his tough, resistant son hard at work.

The father also notices something else as the morning passes: His cheerful, willing, enthusiastic son has not shown up. The day passes and his compliant, Eddie Haskell-like son never comes out to share in the labor. The father begins to figure out that this son who promised to be out in the field sharing the load never intended to come at all.

Making the Connection

1. Describe a time you met a person who was like the second son in an Eddie Haskell sort of way. How do you feel when you are around people like this?

Knowing and Being Known

Read Matthew 21:28 – 32

The God of the Dinner Table

In writing about this parable, pastor Earl Palmer gives some very valuable insight. About the first son he says, "The first son might be described as a big problem at the breakfast table but a great joy at dinner time." Later he makes this observation, "The second son was a joy at breakfast but a big problem at supper." What we have to understand is that this parable is a parable about dinner time! That's what really matters.

Like the first son, we need to face the reality that it is tough to follow the calling of Jesus Christ. We all have moments in which we have to admit that we struggle. None of us has an easy road when it comes to walking and growing in holiness. It reminds me of a prayer I once heard:

Dear Lord, so far today I am doing all right. I have not gossiped, lost my temper, been greedy, grumpy, nasty, selfish, or overindulgent. However, in a few minutes I will be getting out of bed. After that I will need a lot more help. Amen!

We all need help as we seek to honor the Father by saying yes and then living out this commitment with sincerity.

2. What do you learn about the heart of each son as you read the parable?

3. After finishing this short parable, Jesus compares the first son to one group of people and the second son to another group (verses 31 – 32). What comparisons does Jesus make?

4. What is one area in your life in which you struggle with spiritual insincerity: outwardly saying yes to God but not living out your words?

Step #1 toward Spiritual Sincerity: Confrontation

As Jesus is applying this story, he reminds his listeners that John the Baptist came in the way of righteousness and confronted people. People came to John the Baptist to be baptized as a sign of repentance because they were aware of their sinfulness. But the religious leaders defied John, who greeted them with the words, "You brood of vipers." This is the ministry of confrontation. John's words were not designed to ingratiate him to these religious leaders. He told them they needed to bear fruit that was worthy of repentance. He let them know they needed to change, repent, turn around, and go the other way.

Later on, John the Baptist ministered in the same way to King Herod, who was governor over Israel. Herod had taken his sister-in-law away from his brother to be his own wife. John was the only one who confronted Herod on this. He told him that what he was doing was wrong in God's eyes and that it would lead to judgment.

Herod lived with a strange tension. He respected John and liked to listen to him teach, yet at the same time he feared John and was troubled by his teaching. In the gospel of Mark we learn that Herod knew John was a righteous and holy man. He also realized that his own life was out of line, but a part of him resisted this confrontation. Sadly, Herod ended up ordering John's execution after being manipulated and tricked by Herodias.

5. There are times when God needs to confront us and wake us up to our need for repentance and change in our lives. Tell about a time when God confronted you through *one* of the following avenues:

☐ Through the conviction of his Word, the Bible

☐ Through the Spirit working in your heart in a time of corporate worship

☐ Through the words of an unbeliever

☐ Through a trusted brother or sister in Christ

☐ Through some other means

6. Think of someone in your life who loves Jesus deeply and whom you trust enough to let him or her speak words of confrontation and conviction into your life. Describe how God uses this person in your life and you in this person's life.

Step #2 toward Spiritual Sincerity: Response

We are in danger when we become like the second son in this parable, when we give insincere and superficial compliance. This is when we claim to want to do the Father's will and smile as we say yes, but know that we have no intention of living it out. The second son's compliance and words of agreement were only a device to avoid confrontation and pain. We need to be careful that this is not happening in our spiritual lives.

I am thinking of the Christian who comes to church and sings, "Have your own way, Lord. Have your own way," at the top of his voice. He continues: "You are the Potter, I am the clay," but if anyone in his house tries to get the remote con-trol out of his hand, the clay will get pretty hard. For people like this, the number one tactic is confrontation avoidance. Growth will never happen in our lives until we value facing truth more than avoiding pain.

When we are ready to face the truth and live with the pain, we enter the point of response. This is when we say, "God, I see my insincerity and my fear of confrontation. I am ready to face it, with your strength. Give me the courage and power I need to respond to your loving confrontation. Lord, I am ready to change."

7. Once we have been confronted with the truth, we can resist or respond. Tell about a time you were confronted by the truth and responded in a way that brought you back into the vineyard of the Father.

8. In question four you noted a very specific area in which you struggle with spiritual insincerity. What might be standing in the way of your responding to God's leading toward repentance in this area? And how can your Christian friends pray for you and help you over these hurdles?

Step #3 toward Spiritual Sincerity: Transformation

When we look at the ministry of Jesus we begin to realize that he was a genius at the process of bringing about spiritual transformation. He confronts us with the truth about ourselves, elicits a response, and then calls us into an ongoing process of transformation.

Think of Jesus' relationship with the tax collector Zacchaeus. It is pretty clear which of the seven deadly sins had a grip on his life — greed. So Jesus comes to the tree where Zacchaeus is hiding, confronts him, and tells him the truth about himself. Zacchaeus invites Jesus to his home and, by Christ's grace, Zacchaeus is immediately changed. This transformed lifestyle becomes the antidote to greed! He goes on to pay back everyone four times what he overtaxed them. After that, he gives away half of his wealth. Can you see how this disciplined plan of giving might change Zacchaeus's addiction to the wealth of this world? Disciplined actions that bring us into compliance to the will of the Father radically transform our lives.

9. This parable is about the comparison of words and actions. One son says no, but goes to work in the fields. The other says yes, but never shows up. What would you say to a person who makes this claim: "I am truly sorry about a specific sin in my life. I have asked for forgiveness and I feel really bad about it. But I have no intention of stopping. I will continue in this sin."

10. Consider again your area of spiritual insincerity. What transformation and change needs to happen for you to walk in spiritual sincerity and live a life of obedience to the Father?

How can your Christian friends keep you accountable to seek this kind of transformation in the coming days?

Celebrating and Being Celebrated

Close your study by praying for God to fill you with a hunger for spiritual sincerity. Pray for real transformation to happen in your life, especially in your area of struggle.

Loving and Being Loved

If a family member or close friend has confided to you their own battle with spiritual insincerity, take time in the coming days to pray for them and personally encourage them as they seek to grow in this area of life.

Serving and Being Served

Transformation takes time and deep commitment. It involves developing new disciplines and inviting the Spirit to gradually bring change. If you have identified an area in which you feel called to grow in spiritual sincerity, humbly pray about one person who might be able to support you in the process. It might be a person who has modeled maturity in this area of his or her life over time. Allow this person to serve you by communicating your sense of call and by asking him or her to pray for you and help you grow.

THE
PRACTICES
of JESUS

Bill Hybels

Christian Etiquette

LUKE 14:7 – 14; 18:9 – 14

WE'VE ALL BEEN TO BIG BANQUETS BEFORE. WE CAN PICTURE THE SCENE: A chandelier-lit ballroom, lots and lots of tables, each one with a number prominently sticking out of the floral centerpiece, sometimes with name cards already at every chair. As the punch reception comes to an end and the ballroom doors open, guests begin to file in and meander about until they find their seats.

At the front of the room there's typically a special table, usually on a riser to elevate it from the rest, adorned with even fancier decorations, and often with a podium located firmly in the middle. We all know that it's the table reserved for the guests of honor: the wedding party, the company suits, the distinguished out-of-town speaker, or the well-known celebrity and his or her entourage.

Now imagine you decide as you enter the ballroom that you are going to sit at the special table—even though you're not among the guests of honor. Why, you ask yourself adamantly, should you not be served dinner first and have the best view of the proceedings? Why shouldn't everybody be looking at your sparkling countenance instead of those of the bride and groom or Mr. Chief Executive Officer? You're every bit as important as they are. And so up the riser stairs you ascend and down you plop.

Of course, a few minutes later the bride and groom or Mr. Chief Executive Officer and his spouse arrive. Can you guess what will happen next?

Making the Connection

1. Describe what you think will happen next in this banquet scenario.

Knowing and Being Known

Read Luke 14:7 – 14

2. What are the rules of etiquette that come up in this passage?

What are some possible spiritual issues or lessons we find behind the rules of etiquette Jesus addresses?

The Danger of Presumption

Why is Jesus so concerned about protocol around tables and etiquette at meals? Is he really worried that one of his followers might get a wrong seat and then be asked to move to a different table? Is the Son of God all that concerned that one of his disciples would get the public recognition of being asked to come up to the head table after choosing to sit near the back of a banquet room? Is this really what Jesus is getting at with these rules of etiquette? Or, is there something deeper going on here?

As was often the case, Jesus was using an ordinary occurrence or life situation as an opportunity to teach a profound spiritual lesson. If we take note of the setting of this story (Luke 14:1), we discover that Jesus was eating a meal in the house of a prominent religious leader. We also see that the people there were watching Jesus closely. What they did not notice was that Jesus was watching them too. He saw that as each guest entered the room they looked for the most prominent and best place to sit. They wanted to be noticed. They were focused on self-promotion. They were all about themselves. They were committing what can be called "the sin of presumption."

The issue was not the position of the seating chart, but the condition of their hearts. These guests wanted the best position and were ready to take it for themselves. They also had no concern for anyone else at the wedding banquet. Jesus was addressing a social presumption, but on a deeper level he was pointing out the problem with spiritual presumption. This comes when people become so obsessed with self that they actually believe they deserve a seat at every head table and recognition wherever they go.

Read Luke 14:7 – 10 and 18:9 – 14

3. How does each of these passages reveal a spiritual presumption of superiority?

How does God respond to this condition of the heart?

4. What are some of the ways people self-promote in our day and age, and how does this reflect a problem on a deeper heart level?

5. Two signs that presumption is growing in our hearts are: (1) a feeling of being a little (or a lot) better than other people, and (2) an effort to constantly promote ourselves at the expense of others. What are some of the possible consequences of living with presumption in our hearts and actions in *one* of the following areas?

☐ Among siblings in a family system

☐ In a marriage

☐ In the workplace

☐ In the church

☐ In a neighborhood

☐ On an athletic team

☐ On a school campus

The Wisdom of Humility

I play a little game occasionally just to help keep my life in perspective. I don't do this out loud, but quietly, in my heart. I call it "Where Did You Get That?" It goes something like this. I say, "Bill, it's time to make a list again. What do you have and where did you get it?" To start the game I begin to make a list:

- *My life*, where did I get this? It is a gift from God.
- The *breath I just drew in*, where do I get the air? God made it.
- Where did I get the *abilities* I have to teach and lead? These are gifts of the Spirit.
- How did I end up with such an extraordinary *wife*? Only God!
- I have *two healthy kids*, where did I receive such family blessings? From the hand of a loving God.

- The *church* I serve, how did I receive this privilege? Only from Jesus, the head of the church.

I can keep playing this game for a long time, and the answer to every one of my questions is always the same.

After I have played for a while I ask myself, "What do I have to brag about? What could I possibly be haughty about? Why should I deserve a position of honor?" In these moments I am struck by the overwhelming reality that I am a recipient of God's grace in every way possible. I come to a place of healthy and profound humility because I not only get a clear picture of who God is and who I am, but I begin to see the people around me in a new light.

Read Luke 14:11 and Philippians 2:3 – 8

6. Make a list of ten things you have that you greatly value (abilities, material goods, relationships, etc.):

-
-

-
-

-
-

-
-

-
-

Then take a moment to play the "Where Did I Get It?" game, honestly reflecting on the source of each of these valued possessions. How does the discovery impact the way you see yourself and the people around you?

7. Jesus called us to humility and became the best example in history of what choosing the way of humility looks like. What are some specific and practical ways people can "take a lower seat" and put others first?

What might happen if we actually took this invitation seriously and lived it out on a daily basis?

8. Consider a life situation in which you believe God is calling you to humble yourself and take a lower seat. What specific action could you take, and how can your Christian friends encourage you as you grow in humility in this way?

Making Room for the Marginalized

We have seen that there is specific etiquette for guests at a banquet. Next, Jesus addresses another issue: the proper etiquette for hosting a lunch or dinner party. Who should be on the invitation list? Jesus' answer is radically countercultural, almost absurd. He says: Don't invite all the people you would normally invite; rather, invite the poor, hurting, and marginalized. He notes the people groups in his time that would have always been last (or never) on the guest list. Then he says, "These are the people you should invite first."

Remember the context of this whole teaching experience? Jesus is sharing a meal at the home of a prominent religious leader and has noticed that every guest had something to offer to the host. (Invitations to these dinners had a real give-and-take feel to them.) But again, Jesus is moving us past a physical example to a spiritual reality. God has a special place in his heart for the broken and marginalized in society. He cares about them and he wants us to care too. If we live by the world's system, we will never care for the outcasts because they have nothing to offer us in return. But if we live by God's system, we will care, love, and serve everyone — even those who don't care, love, or serve back.

9. Passages in both the Old and New Testaments reveal a special place in God's heart for those who are poor, broken, abandoned, and living on the margins of society. Why do you think God feels so deeply for these groups of people?

Why does God call his followers to feel love and compassion for the marginalized and to take action on their behalf? What can get in the way of us caring and taking the action that we should?

10. Just as there were specific groups of people who lived on the margins of society during Bible times, so there are today. Who are some of these groups of people now?

How can we reach out to these people and extend an invitation into: our hearts, our homes, our church, our circle of friends?

Celebrating and Being Celebrated

When we think of the outcast, the broken, the marginalized, and the "sinners" of society, we should think of ourselves. In God's sight, we are all broken without his grace. There was a time when we were separate from God. Reflect on this reality from Ephesians 2:12–13:

> Remember that at that time you were separate from Christ, excluded from citizenship in Israel and foreigners to the covenants of the promise, without hope and without God in the world. But now in Christ Jesus you who once were far away have been brought near by the blood of Christ.

As you pray today, thank God for what he has done to include you, embrace you, and invite you into his family. Then, pray that God will so fill your heart that you are ready to love the outcasts of this world the way he loves you.

Loving and Being Loved

One way to keep your perspective right is to periodically remember that all you have is a gift from God. Put a weekly reminder on your calendar for the coming month to play the "Where Did I Get It?" game, and then be sure to follow through. If someone happens to notice your calendar notation and asks about it, explain how you are learning that all you have is a gift from God and that this knowledge brings both thankfulness and humility in how you relate to others.

Serving and Being Served

As an individual, family, or small group, identify one way you can work together to serve a person or a group that has been marginalized. Try to steer away from giving money or anything that feels passive. Look instead for a ministry opportunity that will move you into action and get you in proximity and relationship with someone who has been marginalized.

Back to Basics

LUKE 14:25 – 33

AT TIMES IN LIFE THE BEST POSSIBLE COURSE OF ACTION IS GOING BACK TO THE basics, moments when the fundamentals and foundational issues need to be returned to center stage. The great Green Bay Packers football coach, Vince Lombardi, was famous for standing in the middle of his players with a football in hand and beginning a speech, "Gentlemen, this is a football." You can't get more basic than that. Some people have the ability to distill information down into its most essential elements. Here are a few more examples from Coach Lombardi:

Once you learn to quit, it becomes a habit.

If you'll not settle for anything less than your best, you will be amazed at what you can accomplish in your lives.

It's not whether you get knocked down; it's whether you get up.

If you aren't fired with enthusiasm, you'll be fired with enthusiasm.

Similarly, there were times in Jesus' ministry when he made a point of taking people back to the basics. In these moments he would speak with such precision and clarity that the people around him knew exactly what it meant to be his follower. In these moments people had to decide, "Am I really ready to follow Jesus?"

Making the Connection

1. Briefly make your own list of what you believe it means to follow Jesus. What are the top five or six things Jesus expects of those who call themselves a Christ follower?

How do you think Jesus would finish the following statement if he were sitting with you right now: *One of the most important things I want to see my followers do today is . . .*

Knowing and Being Known

Read Luke 14:25 – 33

The Three "R's"

In the message recorded in Luke 14, Jesus gets back to the basics. At the start of the passage we read that large crowds were following him. Jesus was not always a big fan of crowds, knowing that many were coming to hear him teach only because it was the popular thing to do. In fact, whenever he clarified what it truly meant to follow him, many in the crowds left. And that's exactly what happened in this instance when Jesus addresses the three R's.

For many years Americans talked about the three R's (colloquially referred to as reading, 'riting, and 'rithmetic) as the basics of a solid education. Here in Luke Jesus spoke about the three R's that are basic to anyone who wants to be his follower. They deal with: relationships, responsibility, and resources. If we can get these right, we will be well on the way to growing into maturity as Christ followers.

2. What does Jesus teach about each of the following topics in this message:

- Relationships (verse 26)

- Responsibility (verse 27)

- Resources (verses 28–33)

Imagine you were one of the people in the crowd who had just begun following this increasingly popular rabbi. How might you have responded to these three challenges?

3. In your time as a follower of Christ, how has your faith in him impacted *one* of these areas?

☐ How you see your relational life

☐ What you are willing to sacrifice

☐ How you view and use your resources

Relationships: Who's Number One?

The first "R" is relationships. In this passage Jesus says that unless we "hate" our family members and even our own life we can't follow him. These words bother a lot of people. The word *hate* really throws them for a loop. "Hate" here does not mean that we should dislike or have bad feelings toward our family. In other portions of the Bible we are instructed to love our spouse and children; in the Ten Commandments we are called to honor our parents; all through the Scriptures God teaches that we should love our brothers and sisters.

What Jesus means is this: if we are going to be his follower, we must understand that only one relationship in the entire universe demands our ultimate allegiance. Only one relationship can be absolutely preeminent in our life, and that is our relationship with Jesus Christ. Our love for him should be so pure and our devotion to him so passionate that all other relationships — spouse, children, parents, brothers, sisters, our closest friends — pale in comparison. For a fully devoted follower of Christ, our greatest priority is always God and the focus of our heart is Jesus. Nothing else comes close to comparing.

Read Luke 14:25 – 26 and Luke 8:19 – 21

4. What helps you keep Christ at the center of your life and the primary passion of your heart?

What are some of the things that can tend to creep in and try to take first place instead?

5. How can an inappropriate allegiance to another person get in the way of our following and obeying God?

What sacrifices might we have to make by choosing God's will instead of the wishes of another person?

6. As followers of Christ we are called to put Jesus before family members, friends, and every other relationship. If we hear this call and pursue God as our first passion, how might this impact *one* of the following?

- ☐ Our ability to be a spouse who loves and serves faithfully
- ☐ Our effectiveness in being a parent who points our children toward Jesus
- ☐ Our capacity for honoring parents all the days of their lives
- ☐ Our consistency in being a friend who gives godly encouragement and wisdom
- ☐ Our passion for sharing the message of Jesus with people who are spiritually searching

Responsibility: Discovering My Part in God's Kingdom

The second "R" is responsibility. Jesus speaks these words on his way to Jerusalem where he will die on a cross and give his life for the world. This was his mission, his primary responsibility. Listen to his words: "For God did not send his Son into the world to condemn the world, but to save the world through him" (John 3:17) and "For even the Son of Man did not come to be served, but to serve, and to give his life as a ransom for many" (Mark 10:45). Jesus took his calling very seriously.

Every believer in Jesus, every true disciple, will be given a mission, a calling, a responsibility that has kingdom implications. Jesus carried a cross for us and he calls us to carry the cross for his sake. Jesus saw the crowds and wanted them to know that following him would cost something — it would cost everything.

Read Luke 14:27 and Luke 9:23 – 27

7. Following Jesus involves sacrifice. The picture of carrying the cross would have brought vivid images to first-century believers. They knew what a brutal and humiliating experience it was to be executed on a cross. Think about three specific realities that would come with carrying a cross. How have you experienced these as you have walked with Jesus?

- The *weight* of the cross: What burdens and loads has God called you to lift as you follow Jesus?

- The *seriousness* of the cross: How has following Jesus brought a sobriety about the spiritual needs and realities in our world?

- The *pain* of the cross: In what ways have you endured pain, sorrow, or struggle because you have willingly followed Jesus?

8. Part of the responsibility of carrying the cross is putting down some things that we can't keep carrying if we are going to take up the cross. As a follower of Christ, what are some of the things Jesus has called you to put down so you can follow him fully?

Picking up the cross is about taking the responsibilities God places on your life. What are some responsibilities you live with that you would have never had if you were not a follower of Christ?

Resources: Be Ready to Relinquish Them

The third and final "R" in this message is about how we handle our resources. Jesus calls his followers to take a serious account of all we have. Once we acknowledge our every possession, we are to come to his throne and lay them all down. That's right . . . everything. This is part of discipleship.

It is important to note that the Bible is not teaching that possession of material goods is wrong or sinful. Jesus is not saying that every one of his followers should sell all they have and live in a commune. When Jesus says to "give up" everything he is calling us to relinquish it all to his purposes and plan. He calls us to be good stewards of what he places in our care. We are to love God, not the stuff of this world. If we can learn to use resources for God's kingdom and refuse to let money and possessions become a love in our life, we are well down the road to being his disciples.

Read Luke 14:28 – 33; Luke 16:13; 1 Timothy 6:10; and Hebrews 13:5

9. What are some of the indicators that we might still be in love with money and material things?

Why is the love of money such a powerful force in our society and lives?

10. Do you see some hope-filled signs that God is setting you free from the love of money, that the grip and power of possessions is being broken in your life? What are they?

11. What are you trying to do to strike a healthy and Christ-honoring balance between owning possessions and letting your possessions own you?

How do generosity and giving factor into creating this balanced lifestyle?

Celebrating and Being Celebrated

The first "R" is about keeping our relationship with God first, above all human relationships. Meditate on the greatness of God's love for you. Think about all he has done, and continues to do. Then, as you close this study in prayer, thank him for:

- His great love
- His desire to be in a relationship with you
- Opening the way to restored intimacy through the sacrifice of Jesus
- All of his provisions

Loving and Being Loved

Sometimes we try to de-cross the cross. We can be tempted to want Jesus but not want to bear his cross. Take time in the coming week to meet with Jesus and make a fresh commitment to follow him, no matter what the cost. You might want to pray, "Lord, you bled and died on a cross. I am ready to take up your cross each day. I know it will be painful at times. I am sure it will get heavy. I am aware that following you is serious business. I will carry whatever weight you want me to carry. Here is my life. Take me. Use me." Give God the one gift no one else in all the world can give him: your devotion, your life, and your heart.

Serving and Being Served

As we bear the cross of Jesus we hear his call to service. Every follower of Christ is filled with the Holy Spirit and gifted for ministry. Unfortunately, many people in the local church are much more comfortable receiving than giving when it comes to ministry. We are often uncomfortable with the idea of offering our resources for God's work. Commit to a new level of service by offering God two things in response to what he asks of you. First, devote yourself to the responsibility of ministry. Find some way you can serve in your church or community. Second, offer your resources to be used for God's purposes in this world. Hold nothing back.

Lessons from Lazarus

LUKE 16:19 – 31

THERE ARE CERTAIN TIMES IN LIFE WHEN PEOPLE BECOME THOUGHTFUL, introspective, and naturally ponder the purpose and meaning of life. One such time is when we stand next to a casket. Have you been there? It could be a funeral, a visitation, or a graveside service, but something about these moments takes us to an instant place of sober reflection.

Jesus told all kinds of stories and taught countless lessons. Often the images he used were cheerful and uplifting: a shepherd who finds his lost sheep, lilies of the field, birds of the air, a good and generous Samaritan.

Jesus also addressed hard truths through stories. One day he told a story about two funerals. But Jesus did something no one else could do: he pulled back the veil of eternity and gave a glance into the afterlife. Through the story of the rich man and Lazarus, Jesus not only invites us to reflect on the reality of death, but he also helps us learn from what happens after this life ends.

In this study we stand at a gravesite. There are two headstones. One says "The Rich Man" and the other says "Lazarus." Each one lived, died, and has crossed over into eternity. Their lives were dramatically dissimilar, but their eternities are even more different. They both have a story to tell. If we listen, it could impact our life and our eternity.

Making the Connection

1. Why do graveside experiences prompt such deep reflection and sober evaluation of life?

   Tell about a time you attended a funeral, stood by a graveside, or lost a person you cared about. How did reflecting on their passing impact your life?

Knowing and Being Known

Read Luke 16:19 – 31

2. How were the rich man and Lazarus different in life?

   How were they different in death?

3. What do you learn about *one* of the following topics as you read this story?

☐ The potential impact of riches on our attitudes and actions

☐ The reality and nature of heaven and hell

☐ The motivation to share the message of salvation in Jesus

Potential Pitfalls of Wealth

One lesson Jesus is teaching in this story is that affluence can breed excess and insensitivity. Jesus is not saying that it is wrong to have material things. But the attitude of the rich man in the story is heartbreaking. A poor beggar named Lazarus lived right outside the rich man's house and the rich man had to walk past him, almost step over his body, on a daily basis. Lazarus was sick and starving. To make things worse, the dogs came and licked his sores. Yet the rich man never seemed to notice nor did he ever stop to help. He had plenty he could have shared, but the truth is, he did not care.

Sadly, one of the attitudes that can accompany affluence is the expectation and demand for even more wealth. Affluent people can begin to think they deserve the best things in life. It can be a slow and subtle progression, but over time they can become blind to the people around them who have profound needs. The more they focus on what they have and all they want, the less they think about those who have less ... the people they could help and serve.

Read Luke 16:19 – 21; Luke 12:16 – 21; and James 1:17

4. How does God feel about those who hoard what they have and become so insensitive that they don't notice or come to the aid of those in need around them?

5. How have you seen increasing wealth create a growing sense of entitlement?

How can understanding James 1:17 help us overcome a self-centered attitude of entitlement?

6. It would seem that people who have more material resources naturally would be more generous. But the teaching of Jesus and real-life experience teach us that this is not always the case. How can an increase of wealth and the accumulation of material things actually desensitize us to the needs of the poor and the broken in the world?

What can help us open our eyes, heart, and hands to the needy in our world?

The Reality of Heaven and Hell

This story teaches a sobering lesson that many people today do not want to face: there is a real heaven and a real hell, and real people will spend eternity in one place or the other. C. S. Lewis once said, "You have never met a mere mortal." In other words, every person you meet will live forever. The question is, where will they spend eternity?

We don't know exactly what heaven and hell will be like. But the Bible paints enough pictures to assure us that heaven is eternal joy and communion with God and hell is eternal torment and separation from God. That should be enough to wake us up to the reality that people need to hear the message of God's grace in Jesus Christ.

A growing number of people today want to revise the Bible to edit out things they don't like. Certainly a belief in hell is on that list. Some people who call themselves Christians try to argue that the Bible does not teach the existence of hell. They embrace what is called "universalism," the belief that everyone will end up in heaven. The dilemma is that the Bible does not support this man-made belief. We may not like the concept of hell, but followers of Christ don't have the luxury of removing biblical truth just because it makes us uncomfortable.

Read Luke 16:22 – 28; Luke 23:40 – 43; and Romans 8:18

7. How can embracing the biblical teaching of heaven give us hope and strength in the challenging times of life?

8. What would you say to a person who declares: "I can't believe in a real hell because God is loving and would never judge or punish people"?

How can believing in a real heaven and a real hell stir our hearts to share the gospel and love of Jesus with people who are still far from God?

Share the Gospel While You Can

The rich man became an evangelist once he was in hell. At this point he saw the whole spiritual reality unfold. No one had to tell him that heaven and hell were real. But it was too late. He learned that a chasm exists between heaven and hell and no one passes back and forth. Now the rich man wanted to go back and warn his family, but it was too late. What a lesson for followers of Christ. We have this life, and this life only, to reach out to spiritual seekers. We have one life to live and one of our passionate pursuits should be sharing the amazing message of God's love found in Jesus Christ alone.

We also have only one life to show compassion, feed the poor, and care for those who are broken. If the rich man could have done it all over, he might have noticed the needs of Lazarus and offered some food and care.

You might have the spiritual gift of evangelism, and you might not. But every follower of Christ is called to "be prepared to give an answer to everyone who asks you to give the reason for the hope that you have" (1 Peter 3:15). Jesus said that we are to be his light in this world of darkness (Matthew 5:14 – 16). The apostle Paul invited us to become fools for Jesus (1 Corinthians 1:18 – 25). In other words, every Christ follower is expected to get involved in the work of bringing the message of salvation to our lost and broken world through our words and through Christ-honoring acts of compassion.

Read Luke 16:27 – 31; Luke 24:45 – 49; and 1 Corinthians 1:20 – 25

9. If the rich man in this story could stand up for ten minutes in your church some weekend and speak to the people gathered there, what do you think he would say?

10. Why does our world see the message of Jesus as foolishness and those who share the gospel as fools?

Tell about a time you or someone you know had the privilege of being a "fool for Jesus" as the message of grace was shared.

11. What motivates you to share the love and message of Jesus with people who are still far from God?

Who is one person God has placed in your life who needs to come to faith in Jesus, and how does God want to use you as a witness in the life of this person?

Celebrating and Being Celebrated

God did not have to make a way for people to experience forgiveness and grace. He could have left us in our sin. But, in his great love, God sent his only Son to open the door to heaven. All who have received God's grace in Jesus have the assurance that heaven will be their eternal home. As you close, offer up prayers of praise and celebration for:

- The amazing love of God that allowed him to offer his Son as the payment for our sins
- The grace of Jesus that covers our sins
- The reality of heaven and the hope that exists for all who have faith in Jesus
- The privilege we have to share the good news of Jesus with those who are lost

Loving and Being Loved

If heaven and hell are real, one of the greatest acts of love we could ever extend is sharing the message of grace found in Jesus Christ alone. If we love a friend, neighbor, colleague at work, or family member, we will want them to spend this life and eternity in fellowship with God. This means entering into God's plan for reaching the world.

Write down the names of a few people in your life who have not yet started a relationship with God the Father through Jesus his Son.

Commit to pray for some of the following things in the coming month:

- Ask for the Holy Spirit to soften the hearts of these people to the love and message of Jesus.
- Pray for yourself as you seek to serve, love, and communicate the gospel to them.
- Pray for your church to be a place of love and grace where you could invite spiritual seekers.
- Surrender your life to God's will and let God know you are willing to be a "fool" for him if that is what it takes to reach people with the message of Christ.

Serving and Being Served

God wants to see his whole church equipped to share the good news of Jesus and to be passionate about this calling. Consider serving your congregation by introducing a class or churchwide learning experience on the topic of personal evangelism. Two practical tools for inspiring and equipping followers of Christ for outreach are: *Becoming a Contagious Christian* and *Just Walk Across the Room*.

How to Receive a Miracle

LUKE 17:11 – 19

WHAT DO YOU DO WHEN YOU ARE FACED WITH A PROBLEM YOU CANNOT SOLVE?

Where do you go when you experience a disappointment you cannot bear?

To whom do you cry when it feels like life is caving in all around you?

Where do you turn when a relationship is strained and on the verge of falling apart?

When you come to the end of your rope, your resources, and your abilities, what do you do?

The truth is that all of us hit points in our lives when we need a miracle. Sometimes these miracles are the big, amazing, nature-bending moments of God's intervention. God has performed all kinds of miracles throughout history. He has raised the dead, parted seas, rained bread from heaven, given sight to the blind, calmed storms, driven out demons, and fed thousands of people with a few loaves and fishes. Miracles are no problem for God.

But some people define a "miracle" too narrowly. Unless a stone is rolling away from a tomb, the crippled are walking, or the sun stops in the sky, to them it is not a miracle. In this study we will look at the reality that God still does miracles: some of them are nature-breaking invasions of his power, but others are the supernatural interventions of a loving God in our daily lives. God still can and does do both kinds of miracles.

God wants to do miracles, both large and small, in each of our lives. If you have need of God's supernatural intervention to meet a need in your life, you are looking for a miracle. There are times when we face challenges or trials in the workplace and we know the only way we will make it through is with God's power—we need a miracle. There are marriages that are so damaged that only a miracle of God will put the pieces back together. There are financial circumstances that look so hopeless that without a powerful intervention of God there is no way out. Some face emotional struggles that hang like a dark cloud and, without a miracle, no hope appears on the horizon. No matter what we face today, we need to be assured of the fact that God can, and still does, perform miracles!

Making the Connection

1. Describe a time you needed a powerful intervention of God in some area of your life and he showed up in a miraculous way and carried you through.

What is one miracle you need in your life right now, and how can your Christian friends pray with you for this miracle?

Knowing and Being Known

Read Luke 17:11 – 19

2. What was Jesus' part in this miracle involving the lepers?

What was the lepers' part in receiving a miracle from God?

Cry Out for God's Help

The first step in receiving a miracle is coming to God with our need and crying out for help. In this passage we meet ten men who had leprosy, a very real need. They were sick, they were outcasts, and they wanted to be healed. Not one person walks this earth who does not have needs, but the question is, will we cry out to God for help? The lepers in the story expressed their need to Jesus — they cried out for help.

It seems strange, but there are people who need a miraculous intervention of God in their life, but they don't ask for his help. Some people are too busy complaining about their situation. It almost seems they like having something to whine about, preferring to focus on their problems instead of God's possible solutions. Others have given up on life and faith. They won't ask God for help because they think they are in a hopeless situation. These people would love to see their life change, but they are sure that it never will. There are even people who are committed to figuring out and fixing their own problems. They want to be strong and self-sufficient so they won't ask anyone, not even God, for help.

Read Luke 17:11 – 13 and Luke 11:9 – 10

3. Many things can keep people from crying out to God for help. Tell about how you have seen people fail to ask for God's miraculous intervention for *one* of the following reasons:

☐ Because they seem to like complaining about how hard their life is

☐ Because they have become hopeless and discouraged

☐ Because they are committed to figuring things out on their own, without God's help

☐ Because they have asked for help in the past and do not feel God acted the way they wanted

☐ Because their theology says that God does not intervene in our daily lives

☐ Because they believe they are unworthy of God's help and miraculous love

What do you think Jesus would say to this person about his or her reason for not crying out for God's help?

4. What can get in the way of you asking God for help and a miraculous intervention in your life?

What needs to happen for you to come to a place where you will really cry out, in faith, for God's power to be released in your life today?

Receive God's Direction

The second essential ingredient for receiving a miracle is receiving direction from above. When the lepers cried out, Jesus gave them clear and specific directions: "Go, show yourselves to the priests." This might not seem like a big deal to us today, but these men had personal history with the priests. As was the custom, when each of them had begun to show signs of leprosy they would have been brought to the priests to have their skin examined. In each case, a priest had declared them "unclean."

It was the words of a priest that had consigned them to a leper colony on the outskirts of society. It was a priest who had taught them that whenever they approached another person they had to shout out the word, "Unclean!" so people could avoid them. The priests were so concerned about lepers that any contact, no matter how incidental (including having the shadow of a leper touch them), would make them ceremonially unclean.

Now Jesus tells these ten men, "Go show yourselves to the priests." At this point, they were still covered with leprosy. Their condition was likely much worse than when a priest first declared them "unclean" and banished them from the city. You can almost hear the lepers thinking, "You mock us. Don't you think we have experienced enough humiliation? Now you are asking us to walk all the way back into the city shouting 'unclean' every step of the way. Then you want us to visit the priests and hear them explain that we are still not welcome." What Jesus asked of these men would demand courage and faith.

Read Luke 17:14

5. Often when we ask God for a miracle he will call us to enter into the process in some tangible way. He calls us to do something, to take a step of faith. Part of the miracle is that we move into action. Tell about a time you knew God was calling you to take a step of faith that you were reluctant to take.

What happened when you took that step and followed God's leading in that situation?

6. When you feel a prompting to take a step of faith, there are many ways you can confirm that it is God who is leading you, including:

- Testing every prompting and leading against the teaching of the Bible
- Gaining wisdom from mature and godly followers of Christ
- Looking back through your life and the lives of other believers to determine if this leading is consistent with God's work in the past
- Looking back through the history of the church to see that the leading you feel has been experienced by other followers of Christ

How has God used any of these confirmations in a recent step of faith you've taken?

Step Out in Faith

Many followers of Christ have a need and cry out to God for help. They receive direction from him and have it confirmed through the teaching of Scripture. But, in many cases, the miracle dies right there because they refuse to take the steps necessary to follow God.

The ten lepers could have easily stopped right here in the process. They had received the direction, "Go, show yourselves to the priest." It sounded silly, illogical, distasteful, and even humiliating. Why would they ask for another examination of their skin when they could look at their own hands, arms, and legs and see that they were covered with leprosy? Yet, what we read next is one of the greatest phrases in all of Scrip-

ture: "And as they went, they were cleansed." Their faith was demonstrated by taking action on the direction that came from heaven.

One of the greatest needs for Christ followers today is to be able to quietly wait on the Lord so that we can ascertain his direction and leading. Another equally important need is for Christians to have enough faith to say, "I don't care how silly the direction sounds, how illogical it might be. By faith I am going to take the step that God asks me to take." When we can do this with confidence, we are on our way to experiencing God's miracles.

Read Luke 17:14

7. What is the relationship between God's power to do miracles and our willingness to take the steps he calls us to take?

Respond to this statement: All sorts of miracles are never experienced because Christ followers refuse to take the steps of faith God calls them to take.

8. What step of faith has God been calling you to take, but you have been standing still instead of moving ahead?

How can your Christian friends pray for you, encourage you forward, and keep you accountable to take this step of faith?

Express Thanksgiving

What happens when you receive a miracle? What do you do when God supernaturally intervenes and gives a solution, heals a relationship, or provides something you desperately need? How *should* you respond?

The ten lepers in this story paint a vivid picture for us. Nine of them were healed as they journeyed and kept right on the road to the city, straight to the priests to get their dec-laration of cleansing. Who could blame them? This was their ticket back to society, back to a life they had barely dreamed they would ever experience again. But one of the lepers, upon discovering his skin miraculously restored, did an about-face to return to Jesus, giving loud thanks and praise to God as he went. What an example!

Read Luke 17:15 – 19

9. How is it that ten people could experience the same miraculous healing but respond in such different ways?

10. What are some of the things that can cause us to be like the nine lepers and miss opportunities to give praise and thanks to God?

11. What helps you stay aware of God's goodness and work in your life so that you are quick to draw near to him and give thanks?

Celebrating and Being Celebrated

We have all experienced times when God's miraculous power invaded and we have seen him do great things for us or for someone we love. Offer prayers of thanksgiving and praise for the great things God has done in your life. Be like the one leper who came back praising God with a loud voice.

Loving and Being Loved

One of the best ways we can grow in love is receiving God's care through other people. Identify a couple of people in your life who are mature in faith and whom you trust deeply. Use them as a sounding board when you are seeking wisdom in your life direction. Specifically, if you feel God is calling you to specific action, ask for these people to pray and share their insights. Their insights will help you discern when you are hearing God's voice and leading.

Serving and Being Served

God deserves our praise. When we are alone and God does something powerful, we can lift our voice in adoration. But we are also called to lift up praise when we gather together. One of the best ways we can serve the people around us is modeling a heart filled with thankful praise. When God has set us free, given us guidance, or restored us in places of brokenness, we should share these stories of his miraculous presence and power. What miraculous work has God accomplished in your life? Take time this week to share this story with someone else. Tell of God's amazing power and let your story bring hope and inspiration to others.

Becoming a Servant

LUKE 17:7 – 10; 12:35 – 40

TO SAY THAT JESUS WAS COUNTERCULTURAL WOULD BE AN UNDERSTATEMENT of epic proportions. Throughout his life and ministry Jesus questioned the conventional wisdom of his day, cultural and religious norms that everyone took for granted. His teaching stretched people to see life through new lenses, to the point that they did not quite know how to respond. Consider just a few of the radical teachings of Jesus:

> "Indeed there are those who are last who will be first, and first who will be last." (Luke 13:30)

> "For whoever wants to save their life will lose it, but whoever loses their life for me will save it." (Luke 9:24)

> "You have heard that it was said, 'Love your neighbor and hate your enemy.' But I tell you, love your enemies and pray for those who persecute you, that you may be children of your Father in heaven." (Matthew 5:43 – 45)

One of the most striking ways that Jesus called his followers to a revolutionary lifestyle was his teaching on servanthood. Over and over Jesus taught and modeled a life of service.

> Sitting down, Jesus called the Twelve and said, "Anyone who wants to be first must be the very last, and the servant of all." (Mark 9:35)

After washing the feet of the disciples, a dramatic act of service, Jesus said:

> "You call me 'Teacher' and 'Lord,' and rightly so, for that is what I am. Now that I, your Lord and Teacher, have washed your feet, you

also should wash one another's feet. I have set you an example that you should do as I have done for you." (John 13:13–15)

In all four Gospels this message rings out loud and clear. Those who call themselves followers of Jesus are to live the way he did, embracing service as a lifestyle, not just as an occasional recreational activity. Jesus did not simply serve; he lived as a servant. From his humble birth in a stable to his death on a cross between two common criminals, Jesus gave us a picture of what it looks like to serve with humble joy.

Making the Connection

1. Tell about a person in your life who has modeled humble and joyful service.

How have you seen Jesus alive and working through this person?

Knowing and Being Known

Read Luke 17:7–10 and Luke 12:35–40

2. What are some of the ways Jesus modeled the heart and life of a servant?

How is Jesus continuing to serve us—his followers and the church—even today?

3. What do you learn from these two passages about the right attitude and actions of those who follow Christ as servants?

Wrong Motives for Serving

It would be nice to think that everyone who serves does so with healthy motives, but such is not always the case. It is important for us to examine our hearts to make sure we are not serving with the wrong motives.

Some people serve as *an effort to gain God's favor and love.* They believe that if they offer an occasional humanitarian gesture or engage in a few religious endeavors they will get a few points with "the Big Guy in the Sky" and that he will look kindly on them at judgment day.

Some people serve *for human applause.* Wanting recognition and praise from a peer group, they look for things they can do that people will notice and applaud.

Some people serve *for "self-actualization."* Their driving force and goal is to bolster a sense of positive self-esteem. They want to feel good about themselves, to believe they are worthwhile and valuable persons. So they serve others, but in reality, they are being self-serving.

Many people serve in an effort *to appease their sense of shame and guilt.* They might have wronged people in the past and their service is a way of paying penance. They might be wealthy and by helping others on occasion they feel justified living in opulence. Or, they might just be dealing with deep feelings of guilt and they feel better when they do some act of service to help another person.

God loves when we serve, and he understands that our motives are rarely pure as the driven snow. But he wants us to come to a place where we are motivated to serve because we have experienced his love and desire to share it with others.

Read Luke 17:7 – 10 and Acts 20:22 – 24

4. How can serving spin in unhealthy directions when it is motivated by the following?

• An effort to get God's love

• A need to gain the praise of people

• A desire to attain personal fulfillment

• An effort to cover our shame and guilt

5. What are some of the good, healthy, and godly motivations for a follower of Christ to serve?

How can the right motivation shape our service and help us serve for a lifetime?

6. Describe the times you felt you were most naturally and passionately serving for the sake of Jesus. What was happening in your heart, and what motivated you in these times of service?

Rendering Service or Becoming a Servant?

In his book, *Celebration of Discipline*, Richard Foster says, "There is a tremendous difference between rendering service and becoming a servant." Many Christ followers are willing, from time to time, to render service. It can be exciting to go on a mission trip for a week, teach a youth class for a couple of months, serve at a food pantry for a Saturday, or help a neighbor in a moment of need. Most of us are fine with offering an act of service on occasion. But that is dramatically different than becoming a servant.

Rendering service is generally about a short-term foray into the world of serving, done when it's convenient, isn't too demanding, doesn't cramp our style, and if we like the people we are working with. Most Christ followers are willing to serve like this . . . once in a while. But *becoming a servant* gets to the very core of our heart and identity. It is not so much about a project or activity but a disposition of our soul. When we become a servant, all of our actions flow out of this identity.

Read Philippians 2:3 – 8 and John 13:2 – 17

7. How did Jesus become a servant rather than just offering acts of service?

Once Jesus was a servant, how did his actions grow out of this identity?

8. Why is it easier to render acts of service rather than become a servant?

9. If you actually see your core identity as being a servant, how could this impact *one* of the following?

☐ How you feel and respond when someone asks you to help with a task that seems "below you"

☐ How you respond when you have served faithfully and no one says, "Thank you"

☐ How you treat people who have been unkind or selfish toward you

☐ How you serve when no one is around and no one will ever know

Natural and Enthusiastic Servants

The desire to extend humble service to others happens when our eyes and hearts are fixed on Jesus. It just begins to grow from the inside out. When we come to the manger and see the Creator and God of the universe reduced to an infant and born in the stench of a stable, we cannot help but be affected. When we see Jesus, the Lord of glory, stooping down to wash the dirt off his disciples' feet, something in us breaks. We realize that if we had been at that table, Jesus would have washed our feet too (remember, Judas was there and Jesus washed his feet). When we look up at a Roman cross and see the sinless Son of God nailed there, taking the judgment we deserved, the whole world looks different.

We know we are growing into Christ-honoring servants when service comes naturally and with heartfelt enthusiasm. As the Spirit of Jesus lives in our hearts, we find serving is not a chore, a job, or a religious duty but a joy and a passion, a way to identify with our Savior. And, as we serve, we have a profound sense that Jesus takes delight as we reflect his servant-presence in the world.

Read Luke 12:35 – 40

10. How does this passage paint a picture of a person who is ready to serve at all times?

What does it mean to "Be dressed ready for service" and to "keep your lamps burning"?

11. What is an area of service you know God has called you to enter into? (You might already be serving in this area or just aware that God is calling you to serve.)

How can your Christian friends pray for you and encourage you to serve with enthusiasm and joy in this place of Christlike service?

Celebrating and Being Celebrated

Spend time thanking God for his example of humble and passionate service revealed in Jesus. Pray through the life of Jesus as you do this:

- For the incarnation and the way he emptied himself and left heaven for you
- For his birth in a manger
- For a life of ministry and humble service for sinful people
- For giving his life on the cross for your sins
- For the way he sent the Holy Spirit to dwell in you
- For the way he serves you today by protecting, granting power, interceding for you, and so much more

Loving and Being Loved

We all have people in our lives who have modeled what it looks like to be a godly and humble servant. When you watch them there is no sense that serving is a chore or a project; it is just what they do. These people have revealed the presence of Jesus as they have served us. If such a person comes to mind right now, write them a note expressing how God has used them to teach you what it looks like to be a servant. Thank this person for their ministry to you.

Serving and Being Served

Take time in the coming week for a service checkup. Use this study to guide you through three areas of personal evaluation.

1. Review the "Wrong Motives for Serving" box. Do any of these motives drive you? If so, pray for a new attitude and Christ-centered motives for serving.
2. Examine yourself during the week to identify if you are a person who offers occasional acts of service, or if you are becoming a real servant. The truth is, none of us has perfected a servantlike heart. The key is that we are moving away from simply rendering service and moving toward being servants. Where are you on this journey?
3. Are you growing more enthusiastic about serving, and is it flowing naturally from you? Pray that this will happen in growing measure.

Keep Praying

LUKE 18:1 – 8

WE PRAY, AND WE PRAY, THEN WE PRAY SOME MORE. WITH EARNESTNESS AND fervency we lift up our hearts and the needs we carry so deep within us. We cry out in what feels like a ceaseless chorus of supplication as we ask God to hear, to answer, and to intervene. Then, after what feels like endless petition and knocking on the door of heaven, we give up. We tried and it did not work. We were faithful to do our part in prayer every single day for what felt like an eternity ... well, it was six days in a row. But why keep asking when it is clear that God is not going to answer?

Have you ever hit a wall in prayer? If you have, you are not alone. Followers of Christ have been dealing with the motivation for prayer for about two thousand years. For many Christians it is difficult to stay fired up for prayer over the long haul. Why is this? Why don't many of Christ's followers pray more? I believe one big answer is that many people stop praying because they don't think they get their prayers answered enough.

When we pray and receive a dramatic response from heaven, we are motivated to pray more. We think, "God took care of that need; I'll move to the next item on my list." The more answers we get, the more we want to pray. But it works the other way too. If we don't get an answer to a particular prayer, what do we conclude? *Prayer doesn't work. God isn't listening. There is an obstacle I can't figure out. Something's wrong with me. Prayers are answered in other people's lives but not in mine.* When we think this way, we have a tendency to pray less and lose heart. We become faint in our prayers.

Making the Connection

1. What motivates you and keeps you passionate about prayer?

   What discourages you from praying and causes you to shy away from regular and faith-filled prayer?

Knowing and Being Known

Read Luke 18:1 – 8

2. Through the years many people have been confused by this story because they have tried to read it as an allegory. In other words, they try to create a one-to-one correspondence between each element of the story and a spiritual reality. As an exercise in biblical interpretation, reread this parable and draw out the natural and logical conclusions you arrive at if you interpret the judge as God and the widow as us. Just a little warning: you won't like most of the answers.

   If the judge in this story represents God (the recipient of our prayers):

   How does God feel about people?

   Why does God answer prayer?

If the widow represents praying Christians:

How do we get what we want from God?

How does God view us when we pray?

3. The main point of this parable is expressed clearly in the first verse. How does the parable reinforce this central message?

Contrast #1: God Is Not Like the Judge

In this parable we meet a desperate widow who is helpless, penniless, without connections or clout. What a sad beginning. We also meet a despicable judge who is cold to God and heartless toward people. The problem is that the only way this woman will get justice is if the judge grants it, and he couldn't care less! So, what does she do? She bugs this guy so much that he gives her what she wants because he is sick of her. Is this an accurate picture of prayer? Is this the message of Jesus? You might conclude: if you ever want anything from God you will have to bug him until he is so tired of you that he answers your prayer just so you will go away! That is *not* the message of this parable.

Jesus' point is not to *compare* but to *contrast*. In other words, this story is not saying "God is like the judge" but "God is nothing like this judge." What is being contrasted in this story is the issue of inclination. The judge in the story is not inclined to help anyone or offer assistance in time of need. God, on the other hand, *is* inclined to participate in the lives of his children and help us in our need. His eye is on us, his ear is bent to hear us, his hand is outstretched, and his heart is tender toward his children. Jesus is saying: look at this hardhearted, uncaring judge — God is nothing like him.

Read Psalm 103:1 – 13

4. If God is the opposite of this judge in every way, what do we learn about the following?

   • How God feels about us

   • God's inclination to hear us

   • God's willingness to answer prayer

   How does our theology of prayer change when we shift from comparing God to the judge to contrasting God to the judge?

5. In light of what you learn about God and prayer in this new reading of the parable, what do you think Jesus means when he says, "Always pray and do not give up"?

Contrast #2: We Are Not Like the Widow

In the parable we see that the widow is in a bad way. She doesn't have a chance. But, according to Jesus, she has a secret weapon: the power of pestering. Manipulating the judge with sheer irritation, she finally succeeds in having her petition granted. She gets what she is asking for not because the judge loves her, cares about her situation, or even because he is just — but only so she will leave him alone. If we are compared to the widow in this story, then Jesus is teaching that the only way to get prayer answered is to keep bugging God until he gets sick of us and gives in. Again, this is *not* the message of the parable.

The point, as before, is contrast, not comparison. We are nothing like the widow, who is penniless, powerless, desperate, alone, without connection or hope in the world. For those who follow Jesus, this will never be the case. We are loved by God, embraced as his children. We have free access to the throne room of the Father; his ear is inclined to hear our prayers ... the first time we ask.

Read John 1:12 – 13 and Romans 8:14 – 17

6. If we are nothing like the woman in the parable and she is meant to give us a picture of contrast, what do you learn about the following?

   • How God feels about us when we come to him in prayer

   • What kind of confidence we can bring when we approach God

   • Why God answers our prayers

• How "hard" we have to pray to get God's attention

7. If we really believe God is a perfect loving Father and we are his precious children, how might this impact the way we pray?

Why do you think God chooses to use the image of a loving Father to give us a picture of how he wants to relate to us?

When I Don't Get My Prayers Answered

When we make a specific request of God we don't always know how or when he will answer. But we are called to continue on in prayer even if the way he answers is a mystery to us. Consider the following simple but helpful tool to understand how God answers prayer:

Sometimes God says, "Slow." We tend to subconsciously put a note at the bottom of our prayer requests, "Please answer ASAP." We want everything to fall into place according to our time schedule. But God is not bound by our sense of timing or pressured by our urgency. He sees the big picture and knows there are times when an immediate answer would be exactly what we do *not* need. In these moments God says, "Slow." He teaches us patience and reminds us, "Those who wait on the Lord will renew their strength."

Sometimes God says, "No." We can be shortsighted and fail to see the long-term implications of some of our prayers. God sees everything and knows that we occasionally ask for things that are simply unhealthy. Like a child who keeps asking a parent for more candy, we don't always know what is best for us. As the years pass, a mature follower of Christ will look back on some prayers that received a "No" from God and say, "Thank you, God, for being wise and loving enough to tell me that."

Sometimes God says, "Go." When we pray and the timing is right and the prayer is in tune with the heart of God, we get a green light. God says, "Go." We don't have to pound down his door or say the same thing over and over again. God hears, loves, cares, and is ready to answer our prayers. We all love it when God says, "Go." But his "Slow" or "No" answers are just as much a sign that he is at work on our behalf.

Read James 4:1 – 3 and Isaiah 40:31

> Yet those who wait for the LORD
> Will gain new strength;
> They will mount up with wings like eagles,
> They will run and not get tired,
> They will walk and not become weary.
>   (Isaiah 40:31, NASB)

8. What are some of the challenges we face when God says, "Slow," and we have to walk through a time of waiting?

How does God use times of waiting to strengthen and grow us as his followers?

9. In his love, there are times God says, "No." What are some of the reasons God might answer one of our prayers with a loving but firm "No"?

Tell about a time God said "No" to one of your prayers and later, when you looked back, you were so thankful that he did.

10. Many followers of Christ have been wrongly taught that God is compelled to always say "Yes" to our requests. Imagine a parent who always told their toddler "Yes" no matter what the request. What would happen to this child?

God is a loving Father. How is his commitment to wisely tell us "Slow," "No," and "Go" more grace-filled than just answering "Yes" to every prayer?

11. What prayer are you regularly praying right now, and how might your Christian friends support and encourage you as you await God's answer?

Celebrating and Being Celebrated

Praise God for answered prayer and lift up those requests, including the one you noted in question eleven, for which you still await his reply.

Loving and Being Loved

God is a loving Father, our heavenly Abba. He cares more about us than we can begin to understand. Take time in the coming week to thank God for being your Father in heaven. Let him know that you trust his wisdom, even when he says "Slow" or "No."

Serving and Being Served

What prayers of family members or Christian friends are you currently aware of? Consider serving these loved ones by lifting additional prayers on their behalf. As appropriate, write them a note or give them a call to encourage them this week.

THE
PASSION
of JESUS

Bill Hybels

Power Transfusions

LUKE 22:7 – 23, 39 – 46

IN HIS AUTOBIOGRAPHY THE LATE NELSON MANDELA WROTE OF THE TWENTY-seven years he was imprisoned because of his efforts to overturn apartheid in South Africa. Many of those years he was confined on Robben Island in Cape Town Harbor. There the prisoners were forced to perform terrible kinds of manual labor intended to demoralize them and crush their spirits.

After over two and a half decades of incarceration and attempts to silence his voice, Mandela emerged stronger, more passionate about freedom, and ready to press on. He eventually saw the end of apartheid and became the first president (1994 – 1999) of South Africa to be elected in a truly democratic fashion.

When Mandela reflected back on what carried him through those grueling years in prison, and what protected his spirit from being crushed, he came to a simple conclusion: it was the strength he drew from community with other people. Mandela said it was a fatal error in judgment to let the prisoners spend time together. They drew an infusion of power from each other and it kept them alive, brought them hope, and led to the fall of one of the most evil systems of government in human history.

There is power in community. All of us know the strength we draw when we are in healthy relationship with a band of brothers and sisters. God has made us to be in relationship with each other and we draw great strength through community. In Ecclesiastes 4:9 – 12 we read:

> Two are better than one,
> because they have a good return for their labor:
> If either of them falls down,
> one can help the other up.

But pity anyone who falls
and has no one to help them up.
Also, if two lie down together, they will keep warm.
But how can one keep warm alone?
Though one may be overpowered,
two can defend themselves.
A cord of three strands is not quickly broken.

Jesus lived with the awareness of the power of community from eternity past, and he fleshed it out when he was on this planet. When Jesus was on earth he talked about interdependence; he taught about mutuality. When he started his ministry, he selected a small group of men to be his apostles. He poured himself into this band of brothers. They shared life together on the deepest levels. With time, a core group of men and women became like family to Jesus. In everything he did, Jesus made it clear that we can draw regular power infusions through being connected with the people the Father places in our lives.

Making the Connection

1. Tell about a time when your close relationship with a group of people became a source of power and strength in an uphill battle you faced. Or, describe a time you were isolated and distant from others and felt this lack of community weakened you as you faced an uphill time of life.

Knowing and Being Known

Read Luke 22:7 – 23 and Luke 22:39 – 46

2. In each of these scenes from Luke 22 we see Jesus in critical times. In both cases he has surrounded himself with his closest friends. How did his friends support and strengthen Jesus, and how did they let him down?

3. What role is Jesus asking his disciples to play in these critical moments?

When we realize that Jesus is the perfect and sinless Son of God, what lessons can we learn from his commitment to have people close to him in times of need?

Presence Principle

In Matthew 26:36 Jesus makes a simple request of his friends: "Sit here." Jesus is in the garden of Gethsemane, preparing to face one of his most difficult moments on this earth: the implications of taking the cup that had been assigned to him by his Father. In this time of anticipated sorrow and anguish, Jesus turns to his disciples.

A short time later, Jesus asks Peter, James, and John to go farther into the garden with him. They will get a different assignment. But to the whole group of disciples Jesus asks, "Will you stay here with me now? I want your presence. You don't have to talk. Just sit with me."

This could be called the "Presence Principle." It's a practice that isn't talked about very much these days, but it is just as important now as it was in Jesus' day. It is understanding that we can offer a power transfusion to others by simply being with them. We don't have to give answers, explain suffering, fix problems, or make things right. Sometimes the best thing we can do is just be present.

Read Matthew 26:36 – 46 and Job 2:11 – 13

4. What is the value and help of having people sit with us in times of struggle, need, loss, or sorrow?

Why is silence and simply being with people in these times often more valuable than answers and words?

5. Think of a person in your life who is facing a difficult time and might need the presence of other Christians to surround them. How might you come alongside them and bring the grace-filled presence of Jesus through your presence?

252

The Value of Vulnerability

While in the garden of Gethsemane, Jesus asks Peter, James, and John to follow him farther in. Jesus wants them to listen to his anguish for a few moments, to stay and keep watch with him, to support him in prayer. Then we read some of the most unbelievable words of vulnerability recorded in Scripture. Jesus says, "My soul is overwhelmed with sorrow to the point of death" (Mark 14:34).

That's vulnerability.

The strongest person who ever walked this planet, the second person of the Trinity, is overwhelmed and admits it.

Remember, this is a man speaking to other men. He expresses his sorrow and feelings of weakness. It is staggering!

When we offer courageous self-disclosure to an inner circle of friends, they can care for us in deeper ways. Humble vulnerability allows others to pray for us with a level of passion and intelligent insight that will never come otherwise; it allows them to love us better. When this happens, we can receive a much needed power transfusion that will carry us through our uphill journey.

Read Mark 14:32 – 42

6. What are some of the consequences we might face if we refuse to disclose what is really happening deep in our heart?

• Physical consequences

• Emotional consequences

• Relational consequences

- Spiritual consequences

- Other consequences

7. What are some of the reasons Christians resist being vulnerable at a deep level, and how can we get past these roadblocks?

A Close Circle of Friends

We all live within a broad relational world, ranging from casual acquaintances to very close and intimate friends. Most of us can maintain an outer circle of a hundred or more people who we would put in the "casual acquaintance" category. These are colleagues at work, people in our church with whom we sporadically connect, neighbors, people in various social settings, and others whose lives intersect ours. We know their name, recognize them, smile when we see them, and even carry on brief conversations.

In addition to our acquaintances, most of us have about twenty people in a circle we would call "friends." We spend time with them, laugh together, enjoy each other's company, and share life on a regular basis. We could ask a favor of these people and they would be there for us.

Beyond these two groups, most of us have an inner circle of very close friends. Those who study these sorts of things say that a normal person can maintain only a few relationships in this category. These are the people with whom we share the deepest things of life, who become like family to us.

Jesus modeled this multitiered relational world. He taught the crowds and masses and had large groups of people who gathered around him. He also had the twelve disciples and a smaller group of men and women who walked with him. But within this circle of friends were Peter, James, and John. Jesus invested in them on a deeper level and disclosed to them in an unbarred way. They were his close circle of friends. In the moments when Jesus was going to face an uphill experience, these three friends were usually close at hand.

Read Matthew 17:1 – 3; Mark 5:37 – 43; and Mark 13:3 – 4

8. What role did Peter, James, and John play in the life of Jesus, and what role did Jesus play in their lives?

9. Describe a person in your life who is in the "very close friend" category and how God uses this person to strengthen and empower you in your uphill times of life.

What are some things we can do to be a good "close friend" and a source of God's "power transfusions" for others?

The Ultimate "Closest Friend"

In the garden of Gethsemane the plot breaks down. From a human perspective, the story doesn't end the way we wish it would. We would hope that Jesus' inner circle of friends would succeed with flying colors and become a source of power that carries Jesus through this dark and painful time. We might picture Peter, James, and John hoisting Jesus onto their shoulders and carrying him up the hill he was facing. The overhead camera zooms in on the three friends of Jesus exerting all their strength to support the One who had been such a good friend to them — a classic Hollywood ending.

Sadly, that's not what happened. Jesus' inner circle of friends fell asleep — three times. Soon after this, they all ran for the hills and left him alone. It was not the ending we had wanted to see.

Once the crowds were gone; when the disciples melted away; after Peter, James, and John took off; Jesus was still *not* alone. Ultimately, Jesus had to turn his eyes to heaven and draw strength from his Father. His final and closest Friend was still there, the One who would get him to the top of his uphill journey.

Read Psalm 62:1 – 8 and John 15:13 – 15

10. We live in a world where people can fail us and disappear in our time of need. God offers to be our best friend no matter what we face. What are some of the characteristics of God that make him a great Friend?

11. Tell about a time when the only and final source of strength in your uphill journey was God. How did God show up and infuse you with power that no person could have offered?

Celebrating and Being Celebrated

By God's grace, he has placed people in each of our lives who offer the gift of friendship and encouragement in our uphill moments of life. Take time to lift up prayers of thanks for what these people bring to your life:

- Thank God for your circle of friends who you connect with each day.
- Lift up praise for a person who is in your inner circle of friendship, who shares life with you on a deep level.
- Thank God for being your closest Friend, for being there even when others are not.

Loving and Being Loved

Sometimes the best way we can express love is by allowing others close enough to minister to us. When we exercise vulnerability and share our places of struggle, pain, and sorrow, we invite people to become a conduit of God's love into our life. When we are vulnerable, others can pray intelligently for us, they can sit with us, and they can extend God's love and grace.

During this coming week identify where you are experiencing pain and struggle in your life. Then, prayerfully determine with whom you might be vulnerable. These are not things to be blurted to casual acquaintances, but your friends and inner circle would love to care for you in these times. Share your heart with someone; invite them to pray for you and walk with you in this uphill journey.

Serving and Being Served

Remember occasions that different friends have come alongside you in your times of need. Now identify one friend who might need *you* to come alongside *them*. Contact this person and ask if you can spend time with them. Don't come with an agenda or plan to fix things. Just offer the ministry of your presence. Pray that God will bring his presence through you.

Downward Mobility

LUKE 22:24 – 30; JOHN 13:1 – 17

ANYONE WHO'S BEEN TO HIGH SCHOOL HAS EXPERIENCED THE INFAMOUS SAT (Scholastic Aptitude Test). Below is a much easier SAT: a Status Analysis Test. This test is designed to determine how aware you are of the various status levels associated with certain products and services. Simply circle the answer that holds the most status in the eyes of most people:

1. Which hotel chain has the highest status?
   a. Holiday Inn
   b. Budgetel
   c. Hyatt Regency

2. Which vacation spot has the highest status?
   a. The Peoria KOA
   b. The French Riviera
   c. Six Flags

3. Which golf course has the most status?
   a. Augusta National
   b. Summer Greens Municipal
   c. Bob's Pitch and Putt

4. Which store has the most status?
   a. Kmart
   b. J. C. Penney
   c. Saks Fifth Avenue

5. Which purse label points to the highest status?

   a. Larry's Leather World

   b. Gucci

   c. Nine West

6. Which car make brings the most status?

   a. Ford

   b. Lexus

   c. Hyundai

7. Which watch has the most status?

   a. Seiko

   b. Timex

   c. Rolex

8. Which ink pen has the most status?

   a. Bic

   b. Cross

   c. Paper Mate

9. Which kind of college has the most status?

   a. Ivy League

   b. Community college

   c. State university

10. Which restaurant has the most status?

    a. Burger King

    b. Bob's Big Boy

    c. Ruth's Chris Steak House

This little test demonstrates that most of us are fairly status conscious. We might not think of it on a daily basis, but we are all aware of what says "status" and what does not.

When we meet someone for the first time we can function with an invisible ladder in our mind. The first question is just a formality: *What is your name?* You put the ladder in position. The second question: *What do you do for a living?* Whatever that person says moves them up or down on our imaginary ladder. The next question: *Where do you live?* Another status assessment is made and they move up or down on the ladder. We evaluate the clothing they wear, the car they drive, the jewelry on their hands, wrist, and around their neck. All of these impact where they end up on the status ladder.

We all wish this were not true. On our good days, we don't measure others or ourselves by these status-bearing symbols. But, if the truth be known, we can all slip into these silly games and measurements and place people high or low on our status ladder based on things as arbitrary as the car they drive or the label on their purse.

Making the Connection

1. How do you see people playing the "status game" as they evaluate others based on these arbitrary measurements?

How can people fall into the trap of measuring and judging themselves by these same status-based standards?

Knowing and Being Known

Read Luke 22:24 – 27 and John 13:1 – 17

2. Both Luke 22 and John 13 are accounts of what happened around the table where the Last Supper was celebrated. Imagine Jesus breaking the bread, pouring out the cup, and preparing his followers for the greatest sacrifice in this history of the world—his own body and blood paid as the price for sins. Now, picture the disciples as they begin to debate over which of them would be considered the greatest. Picture them at the table with dirty feet, unwilling to serve each other by offering the customary act of footwashing. How did the behavior of the disciples in both of these passages reveal what was in their hearts?

3. How do the example and teaching of Jesus create a vivid contrast to the prideful and status-seeking attitude of the disciples?

The Problem with Power

Left to ourselves and without the influence of the Holy Spirit in our lives, the vast majority of us would be unbridled status seekers. It is in our blood. It is part of what it means to be conceived and born in sin. Indeed, the very first sin in the garden of Eden was all about ladder climbing. The lie went something like this: "Eat of the tree; you will not die; you will vault up a whole bunch of rungs on the status ladder. You will be like God, at the very top." This struck a chord in the sinful heart of humanity.

Upward mobility excites and entices us. We wish we had the power to control our own fate, the power to control our circumstances, the power to experience all of our wildest pleasures, the power to eradicate the opposition. We convince ourselves that if only we had power we would use it properly; we would exercise it wisely. But if history is any kind of teacher, most of us would not. In fact, usually the old adage holds true, "Power corrupts and absolute power corrupts absolutely." Unchecked power leads to exploitation of the weak, oppression of the poor, self-centeredness, insensitivity, discrimination, injustice, and the list goes on and on.

Read Luke 22:24 – 25 and Genesis 3:1 – 7

4. What are some examples of how power has been misused throughout history?

• In the political arena

• In economics

• In the church (and in the name of religion)

• In homes and families

5. In light of the human tendency toward status seeking and our propensity to abuse power, how do you think Jesus might respond to a person who makes *one* of the following statements?

☐ If I inherited millions of dollars I would use it to help people in need and would be generous with the poor. I would not let it go to my head.

☐ If only we could get our person or party into the position of authority in our government, everything would be all right!

☐ I know that power is a dangerous thing and status can lead to pride, but I really think I can handle it.

The Danger of a Status-Seeking Life

We live in a world where status seeking is accepted, even commended. Pursuing status and climbing the ladder come so naturally to all of us that the idea of intentionally reducing status, descending the ladder, or choosing downward mobility seems bizarre in comparison.

To understand why God is so concerned with upwardly mobile, status-seeking people, we need to see how such behavior impacts the way we see the world and affects our uphill journey of life. When we devote ourselves to status seeking, a number of things happen:

First, we begin to feel we have some kind of intrinsic authority and that God's authority does not apply to us. We believe our will is most important.

Second, we naturally conclude that we are not accountable to God or people. We can live and act in a vacuum, believing there will be no consequences. We feel as if we are the exception to the rules of society and the Bible.

Third, and finally, sin runs wild in our heart and life. Since we have all power and we answer to no one, anything goes. When we hit this point, the negative spiral begins to draw us downward, farther from God each day. Anything and everything seems justifiable.

Read Romans 1:21 – 25 and Luke 22:24 – 25

6. In Romans 1, the apostle Paul paints a picture of human beings spiraling deeper and deeper into sin. As people rebelled against God "he gave them over" to their sinful desires. Self-centered, status-seeking hearts led to all kinds of sinful behavior, and they still do. Why do you think God allows us to make decisions that can hurt others and ourselves?

Why would God "give us over" to the sinful desires of our hearts?

Jesus' Example of Downward Mobility

When we learn to walk closely with Jesus we begin to view power, authority, and status in a whole new way. Jesus was the most powerful Being to ever walk the face of this earth. As he gathered with his followers for the Last Supper he was fully aware of who he was (God), where he had come from (heaven), and where he was going (back to glory). Knowing all of this, Jesus extended one of the most humble acts of service possible: he washed the feet of his followers. Jesus modeled downward mobility.

In Luke's account of the final Passover meal we find the disciples arguing about which of them was the greatest. Jesus reminded them that the Gentiles play the "Who's the Greatest?" game. He called them instead to live a countercultural existence of childlike faith and humble service, to follow his example and choose the pathway of downward mobility.

Read John 13:1 – 17 and Luke 22:24 – 27

7. How did the disciples respond to Jesus' radical act of footwashing? How do you think they felt when they realized they had failed to offer the service of footwashing to each other only to have Jesus step in and do it for them?

8. After washing the feet of the disciples, Jesus taught them (see John 13:12–17). What was the heartbeat of his message, and how does this truth translate to our lives today?

9. Respond to *one* of the contrasts below:

☐ In this world, those who have power are those who are served. In God's kingdom, those with the greatest power are called to serve others.

☐ In the world, the weak and powerless do the grunt work and get the menial jobs. In God's family, those who are strong and able should willingly do humble tasks of service.

☐ In the world, those who are leaders delegate the undesirable tasks to those "under them." In God's kingdom, leaders are the first to serve and exhibit humility as they lift up others.

An Invitation to Downward Mobility

God wants to curb our desire for upward mobility. He actually wants to teach us a new way of thinking that will lead to downward mobility. When this happens, we become obsessed with the status of people's hearts, not their pocketbooks. We care so much that we are willing to serve them and love them whether they are rich or poor in earthly goods, seeing only their needy hearts. We care so much that we are willing to step down so that we can lift them up. This is what Jesus did for us when he left the glory of heaven to be born in the squalor of a stable. It was the ultimate act of downward mobility. Through his teaching and vivid life examples, Jesus is calling his followers to intentional, consistent, and Christlike downward mobility. The evidence that we truly hear and follow Jesus' teaching is simple: we begin to serve others with joy, humility, and passion — we become servants.

Read Luke 22:27; Mark 10:45; and Philippians 2:3 – 11

10. If Jesus were on earth today and wanted to model specific acts of humble service to his followers, what are some things he might do?

11. What is one step toward intentional downward mobility you can take in the coming months, and how can your Christian friends pray for you and encourage you to live more like Jesus as you take this step?

Celebrating and Being Celebrated

If you had been sitting at that table when Jesus washed the feet of his followers, he would have washed your feet too! Jesus has served each one of us in ways we could never repay. Thank God for this truth. Here are a few possible prayer starters:

- Father, thank you for serving us by sending your Son.
- Jesus, thank you for serving us by leaving the glory of heaven and coming to earth.
- Jesus, thank you for serving us through your sacrifice on the cross.
- Spirit, thank you for the way you serve us by bringing comfort in times of need.

Loving and Being Loved

We all are the beneficiaries of those who have modeled lives of humble service. These godly people have lived with gentle humility. They have served with no demand for recognition or public praise. Because they walk with Jesus and are seeking to be like him, they naturally wash feet and serve others, including us!

In the coming weeks, contact two or three people who have taught you, through their lifestyle, what it looks like to live as a servant. Call them, meet with them, send an email, whatever. Let them know that you have seen the servant heart of Jesus modeled in their life. Thank them for how they have helped you learn to be more like him.

Serving and Being Served

People who hold a position of influence, authority, or power have a unique and God-given opportunity to choose downward mobility. Rather than using this place to exalt self or promote personal advancement, we can use it to serve others. Our place of influence can be a platform for lifting up people with needs, hurts, and struggles.

Whether this place of power is in government, the marketplace, the classroom, the church, the home, or elsewhere, we must realize that all authority is derived. At best, the position we currently hold is a temporary entrustment from God to be used for good, for his glory, and for the benefit of people under our care. Remember, we will be held accountable. To whom much is given, much is required.

Reflect deeply on 1 Peter 5:6: "Humble yourselves, therefore, under God's mighty hand, that he may lift you up in due time." Then, think about each life situation you face on a regular basis—home, work, church, social settings, etc.—and pray for the courage to live as a servant.

Grace Under Pressure

MATTHEW 26:14 – 75

I'VE ALWAYS ENJOYED A LITTLE-KNOWN VERSE IN THE NEW TESTAMENT, WRITten by the apostle Paul as a challenge to an inexperienced young leader named Timothy. This budding leader has his whole leadership life in front of him. Of all the possible instruction the seasoned apostle could give to Timothy, one of the most striking things he wrote was: "But you, keep your head in all situations" (2 Timothy 4:5).

These words might not sound all that spiritual when you first read them. As a matter of fact, they have the earthy feeling of simple common sense. Paul is telling Timothy that when things get tough, when the hill gets steep, when you think you are going to lose it: "keep your head." As the years pass, these words have become a deep spiritual truth I have sought to memorize and live out on a daily basis.

There are alternatives to keeping your head in all situations. You can lose your head. This is a strange expression, but we all know what it means. It is far too easy for us to allow our impulses to take over instead of our mind. We can allow anger to flow and our words to cut. We can let our appetites, lusts, and desires run wild instead of making wise decisions. We can let anxiety wreck our life instead of walking in the peace of Jesus. We all know what it means to lose our head because every one of us has done it!

As Jesus walked up the hill to Calvary, all sorts of opportunities for him to lose his head were available. Thankfully, he kept his head in all things. Rather than respond in anger and retaliate with wrath, Jesus showed us what grace under pressure can look like. As we watch the Savior climb his final hill, we too can learn much about living in grace—even in the hard times, especially in the hard times.

Making the Connection

1. Describe a time you saw someone "lose their head."

   What are some of the potential consequences when people lose their head?

Knowing and Being Known

Read Proverbs 25:28; Galatians 5:22 – 26; and 2 Timothy 3:1 – 5

2. Another term the Bible uses for this idea of "keeping our head" is self-control. Why is self-control so important in the life of a follower of Jesus?

   If Christians lack self-control and lose their head on a regular basis, how might this impact the witness of Christ to those who are not yet believers?

When Friends Fail You

When the heat is on, sometimes the people we love melt away. This happened to Jesus. One of his inner circle, Judas, sold him for a handful of silver pieces. Can you imagine a friend actually taking money to betray you? Then, one of Jesus' three closest friends, the apostle Peter, denied him three times. Particularly painful was the fact that Jesus saw and heard Peter as he swore he did not even know the Savior. In addition, all the disciples ran away and deserted Jesus in his time of need.

Read Matthew 26:14 – 16, 20 – 25, 31 – 35, 47 – 50, 56, and 69 – 75

3. What were some of the ways the friends and followers of Jesus let him down during the last week of his life?

How did Jesus model grace even as his closest friends let him down?

4. We all have times when our friends, family members, and those closest to us will let us down. This is just the nature of having relationships with imperfect human beings. When these moments of disappointment come, we can extend grace or lose our head and hurt them back. What are some of the ways we can show grace, like Jesus did, when people let us down?

When Violence Looms Close

When the crowds came to arrest Jesus in the garden of Gethsemane, Peter "lost his head." Peter had walked with Jesus for three years. He had heard many teachings on being a peacemaker and not retaliating in the face of violence:

> "Blessed are the peacemakers, for they will be called children of God." (Matthew 5:9)

> "But I tell you, do not resist an evil person. If anyone slaps you on the right cheek, turn to them the other cheek also." (Matthew 5:39)

> "But I tell you, love your enemies and pray for those who persecute you, that you may be children of your Father in heaven." (Matthew 5:44 – 45)

It is one thing to teach nonviolence and another thing to have a mob attack you. It is one thing to say, "Turn the other cheek," and an entirely different thing to have someone nail you to a cross. It is one thing to talk about praying for your enemies and a radically different thing to hang on a cross and look down at people who are mocking and reviling you. Jesus taught his followers to be grace-filled peacemakers. On his uphill journey Jesus had a chance to show if he would practice what he preached.

Read Matthew 26:50 – 54

5. In the midst of a violent attack, Peter and Jesus responded in dramatically different ways. Peter reached out with a sword and returned violence for violence. Jesus reached out his hand and offered healing. How can followers of Jesus respond with grace and healing when confronted by violence?

When False Accusations Fly

Lies, lies, and more lies. As Jesus continued on his uphill journey he faced another point of battle. False witnesses brought a list of deceitful lies against him. His accusers twisted the truth. They made stuff up. They took his words, misinterpreted them, and claimed he was saying things he never said. Throughout a series of mock trials Jesus had to decide how he would respond to the lies that were leveled at him.

We have all been there. In this world we don't walk far before feeling the sting of hurtful words. People twist what we say. They misrepresent us. They shade or embellish the truth and try to make us look bad. In these moments we can look to Jesus and learn from how he faced false accusations.

Read Matthew 26:59 – 68; Matthew 27:11 – 14; and Luke 23:8 – 12

6. Wave after wave of lies and false accusations came crashing over Jesus as he was taken from trial to trial. What do you learn about responding to hurtful and deceitful words as you observe Jesus' responses?

7. What is your natural response when people lie about you, make false accusations, or slander you?

How can followers of Jesus respond with grace when people are attacking their character and speaking falsely about them?

When Pain Screams

After Jesus appeared in the courts and navigated the sea of lies, things really went south. Next came a barrage of physical attacks so brutal that most of us would have a hard time imagining them. Physical exhaustion must have set in. Jesus had been harassed and shuffled from trial to trial. He went through a merciless flogging with a whip that had pieces of bone and metal embedded in the leather straps. In the process of crucifixion they would often pluck the beard as a form of torture and in an effort to bring public shame. They had forced a crown of thorns onto Jesus' head. He had to carry the cross up the hill. Then, they crucified him.

As unimaginable pain tore through his body, Jesus could have lashed out. He could have retaliated. At the least, he could have launched a few verbal volleys back at the people who were torturing him. He was a man. He did feel the pain. As we look intently at Jesus in the midst of agonizing pain, we can learn how to climb a hill that brings suffering.

Read Matthew 27:26 – 35

8. Jesus was fully human and felt exactly what any person would have felt. He was dying in our place and for our sins—he had to feel what we would have felt. How do you see Jesus ministering grace through the screaming pain he must have endured?

9. None of us will experience the same suffering Jesus did. But we are called to be gracious and loving even when we face pain and suffering. Tell about a person you have known who lived with grace and kindness even while facing physical suffering. What have you learned about hill climbing from their example?

When Needs Are Near

We all love to help people in their times of need. When we feel strong, refreshed, and our tank is full, it is an honor to serve others. But when our tank is empty and we are in need, it is hard to help others. One of the toughest things to do is face a time when we are climbing a steep hill and realize that we just don't have the physical, emotional, or spiritual reserves needed to help carry someone else's load. It is taking all we have just to get out of bed, put on our shoes, and make it through the day.

When Jesus was near the top of his uphill climb, his tank must have been almost empty. He had been through an emotional and spiritual war. His body was ravaged. Almost everyone he loved had betrayed him, denied him, or run away. The crowds were screaming and mocking. In this setting, needs arose. A man on the cross next to him needed grace. His mother needed protection and provision for the future. What do we do when we are depleted but people still have legitimate needs?

Read Luke 23:32 – 43 and John 19:25 – 27

10. As Jesus was suffering and dying, facing the final steps of his uphill journey on this earth, he continued to be confronted by human needs. What do you learn as you watch his response to the thief on the cross and his care for his mother?

11. We all have people in our lives with needs. It might be a friend, child, aging parent, spouse, neighbor, fellow church member, or a stranger who crosses our path. Tell about a time when you were depleted and empty, but you were still called to meet the needs of others. Where did you get the strength and energy to serve even when you felt you had nothing to give?

Celebrating and Being Celebrated

We all have uphill heroes — parents, grandparents, friends, others — who have loved, served, cared, and ministered to us even when they were climbing a steep hill of their own. Thank God in prayer for these people. Then close by thanking Jesus for climbing the hill of Calvary, carrying you in his heart all the way to the cross.

Loving and Being Loved

Jesus calls us to forgive. He does not *suggest* that we forgive or simply *hope* that we will forgive. He *commands* that we forgive with the strongest urgency (Matthew 6:12, 14 – 15; 18:21 – 35). The focus of Jesus' uphill journey was to extend grace to you and me and wash away all of our sins. At the top of his hill was a cross and on that cross our forgiveness was sealed with his blood.

If you have a person in your life who has wronged you, search your heart. Have you forgiven them? Have you asked God to free you from harboring anger, bitterness, vengeance, and sorrow? If not, read the Matthew passages listed above and ask God to teach you the freedom of forgiveness. Or read through Jesus' uphill journey to the cross as a reminder of how he offered grace and forgiveness to those who abused him. Meditate on how he prayed for his oppressors. Be amazed by how he loved his disciples even when they stumbled.

Serving and Being Served

We all know people who face chronic pain and ongoing physical struggles. These brave saints often serve God and people through the fog of their suffering. If you know someone like this, pray about how you might serve them through lifting a burden, helping in some way, or visiting them with the goal of bringing encouragement.

A Full Tank for Hill Climbing

MATTHEW 26:36 – 46; PSALM 22; PSALM 31:1 – 5

WHEN YOU'RE CLIMBING AN EVEREST OF YOUR OWN, FACED WITH AN OVER-whelming and faith-stretching incline, how do you maintain self-control? How do you keep your head? How do you climb a hill like Jesus did?

Here is a brief hint: exerting additional amounts of willpower isn't enough. Though it may help somewhat, willpower will fade long before your adverse circumstances settle down. Personal strength will wane way before your hill becomes flat ground. Willpower alone will not help you keep your head when things are going sideways.

Jesus kept his head in times of pressure. He could do this because his spiritual tank was full. He had fuel for the journey. The key to Jesus' strength can be traced back to a single truth that he taught. It's a simple truth to wrap your brain around, but full of meaning: "A good man brings good things out of the good stored up in his heart, and an evil man brings evil things out of the evil stored up in his heart" (Luke 6:45).

If you can take hold of this spiritual wisdom it will be very valuable as you move forward in your hill-taking adventures.

Like Jesus, we all face hills—financial, medical, relational, vocational, emotional, spiritual, what have you. These hills can be daunting, exhausting, faith stretching. As was the case in Jesus' life, it's not just the hill, but the adversities and aggravations thrown into our path as we navigate our way to the top of it. As the hill gets steep, our energy ebbs, we feel fatigued, and we're tempted to bail. "I've had enough!" we want to cry. Anger, anxiety, and frustration can take over. We can lose our head.

In these times we need spiritual sustenance, the strength that only God can give. We need to have our tank full because the reality is that we burn a lot of fuel while climbing life's steep hills. And the steeper the hill, the faster we burn our spiritual energy reserves. This certainly is true in the physical world. When we run up a steep hill or ride a bike up a significant incline, we run out of energy faster. The same is true when it comes to spiritual fuel. The steeper the hill, the faster our reserves are depleted. When we see that our tank is running low, we need to be wise and refill it. If we don't, we can run out of gas and end up on the side of the road.

Making the Connection

1. At various times of life we face different kinds of challenges. Sometimes the road is flat and smooth and we don't burn much fuel. At other times the road is steep and our tank can run dry quickly.

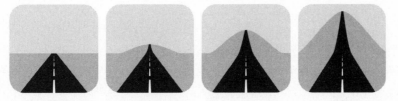

Which road above best represents where you are in your life journey today? If you are climbing a hill today, what kind of hill is it (relational, emotional, financial, spiritual, physical)?

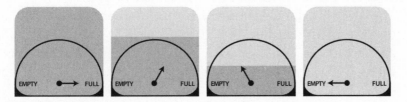

Which tank above best represents the state of your spiritual reserves for hill climbing right now? Why is your tank at this level?

THE PASSION OF JESUS

Knowing and Being Known

2. What sorts of things can help us replenish our spiritual tank to ensure we are ready for any hill that might be ahead?

What tends to deplete your spiritual reserves and drain your tank?

The Strength of Solitude and Silence

When Jesus climbed his hill all the way to the cross he used a lot more than willpower. He had ways to keep his tank full so that he could face any hill that came his way. One of his tank-filling disciplines was making space for solitude and silence. If we take time to read the Gospels closely we will notice how often, sprinkled among the narratives, are phrases such as, "And then Jesus withdrew and went to a quiet place."

In the language of spiritual development this is called solitude: carving out a space in your life where God can speak to you. It is about being quiet, setting aside anxiety, being at the feet of Jesus. When starting to develop a discipline of solitude, it can feel a lot like waiting around for nothing. But in these quiet moments God speaks. He meets us. He fills our tank.

Read Matthew 26:36 – 39; Mark 6:30 – 32; and Mark 1:35

3. The Gospels paint a picture of Jesus making space for solitude as a regular part of his schedule. In particular, when he had to make an important decision he would get away with the Father. What are some of the things God can do in our hearts and lives through times of solitude and silence?

4. Our world is filled with noise and clutter. For many believers, the idea of being quiet is almost a foreign concept. Why is silence so difficult for so many people? Why do we avoid it?

What are some ways we can "turn off" or "unplug" to create space for quiet in our lives?

5. Tell about how you have tried to develop habits of silence and solitude in your life. What has worked for you, and how has God met you in these quiet places?

The Power of Prayer

Jesus filled his tank by making space for silence and solitude. In addition, he knew that one of the best ways to make sure his tank was full was by speaking to the Father in prayer. Indeed, prayer was a regular filling station for the Savior!

When the alarm goes off in the morning, you have a choice to make. You can shoot out of bed and jump into life at full speed. Or, you can quiet your soul and talk with God. Many people are action-oriented and tend to hit the floor running. One simple discipline that can help keep your tank full is this: roll out of bed onto your knees instead. Take a few minutes to be with God. Listen for his voice. Tell him about the hills you are facing. Ask for the Spirit's presence and power to fill you. Surrender yourself to God's plans for the day.

Read Matthew 26:36 – 46; Matthew 27:46; and Matthew 6:5 – 15

6. Prayer played a central part throughout Jesus' life and ministry. What was the role of prayer as Jesus walked his final uphill battle from the garden of Gethsemane to the cross?

7. How can prayer function as a filling station that refuels our tank and prepares us to keep climbing the hills we face each day?

Describe a time you felt depleted and empty only to have prayer fill your tank and empower you to press on.

8. Prayer can refuel us in various ways. Some people use a prayer list to lift up the needs of others. Others pray the Scriptures and let them shape their communication with God. In some cases, songs, hymns, and spiritual songs become soul-filling prayers. Tell about a practice or discipline of prayer that really connects you to God and regularly fills your tank.

Sustained by God's Word

Along with solitude and prayer, Jesus knew how to fill his tank through meditating on the truth of Scripture. He was immersed in the powerful truth of the Bible. He feasted on it and let the words of Scripture empower him as he climbed the hills he faced on this earth. We can learn from his example.

When we feed on the Scriptures, whether or not we're mindful of it, our tank fills. Every line of the Bible is Spirit-breathed (see 2 Timothy 3:16), God's very word to us. Sometimes we can immediately feel the power of what we are reading. At other times it is like eating a good meal — nutrients are filling our body and doing their work, but we really aren't aware of it. The discipline of Scripture reading, memorization, and meditation is one of the best tank-filling activities in the spiritual life.

Read Psalm 22 with Matthew 27:45 – 46 in mind; read Psalm 31:1 – 5 with Luke 23:44 – 46 in mind

9. How does Jesus' knowledge and love of Scripture come to the surface in his uphill journey?

10. How does regular reading and study of the Bible fill the tank of a follower of Jesus?

How does neglecting Scripture reading impact our fuel level and ability to climb hills for God?

11. There are many ways to develop and exercise the discipline of Bible reading, study, meditation, and memorization. Tell about a particular approach to Scripture reading you have used that served to fill your tank and strengthen your faith.

Celebrating and Being Celebrated

God has given us so many ways to fill our tanks and stay refreshed and charged up. Lift up prayers of celebration for:

- The gift of the Bible and for the truth it brings to our lives
- The freedom we have to enter God's presence through prayer in the name of Jesus
- The wonder that God longs for us to sit at his feet in quiet times of fellowship
- Other ways you can draw near to God and be filled with his presence

Loving and Being Loved

Willow Creek Community Church conducted an extensive study of many churches in an effort to discover how Christians can continue growing in their faith. One finding was that the best way for people to keep maturing, at any stage of their spiritual life, is consistent study of the Bible. It is great to listen to sermons, but even better to open your own Bible and dig in.

If you think you can climb your hill on the basis of an hour or two each week in church, you are sadly mistaken. The church was never supposed to be your only refueling time in a given week. We should integrate rhythms and practices of spiritual growth throughout the course of our days. The most important of these is regular Bible reading.

Consider asking a family member or Christian friend to keep you accountable in your personal Bible study. Don't make it a legalistic job to check off your to-do list. Instead, look at it as a joyful privilege to meet with God, feed on his Word, and receive his wisdom and filling.

Serving and Being Served

Over the years I have developed a practice, a simple act of service, which I pass along as a suggestion to you: take time each week to pray for someone you know who is facing a steep uphill journey. After you have done so, send an email message, "Praying for you!"

The Three Crosses

LUKE 23:26 – 43

WE ALL FACE DEFINING MOMENTS, TIMES WHEN WE MAKE A CHOICE OR TAKE a course of action that changes the whole trajectory of our life. With one decision, things will never be the same. With one step, in a particular direction, our life moves on a new pathway. These times, which impact us more than we can possibly dream or imagine, often come as we press forward on our uphill journey of faith.

A man and woman meet and then they build a friendship that blossoms into a romance. Eventually they make an important decision to stand before family, friends, and God to declare, "As long as we both shall live." A whole new history begins.

A young woman thinks and prays about her vocational life. The future is filled with options. Then, with time and counsel from family and friends, she declares a college major, sets her sight on an education degree, and begins the journey of becoming a teacher. This defining moment will impact the next three decades of her life.

A junior high boy is standing outside of a grocery store with some friends. They goad him, taunt him, and finally convince him to walk in, take a couple bags of candy, hide them under his coat, and walk out without paying. As he walks into the store, he is facing a moment that could redefine his future.

A high school girl who has never been in the party scene is out driving around with her friends. They stop in a local park and convince her to join them as they drink a few beers. She feels different, but still believes she is in control and will have no problem driving herself and all her friends home. They return to the car and she gets ready to start the car. This could be a defining moment on many levels.

Two men, placed on trial for the crimes they have committed, are found guilty. The sentence: death by crucifixion. Each is nailed to a Roman cross and suspended in the air for everyone to see. Between them is a man named Jesus, also hanging on a cross. The word on the street is that this Jesus is a miracle worker, a religious teacher, maybe even the long-awaited Messiah. This is the ultimate defining moment. The decision each man makes in the next couple of hours won't just impact what is left of their lives; it will determine their eternities.

Making the Connection

1. Describe a defining moment when you made a decision (for better or for worse) that had a dramatic impact on your life.

Knowing and Being Known

Read Luke 23:26 – 43

2. Luke records three things Jesus said as he hung on the cross. Note his words to *each* of the following people and the message you hear in his words.

   • The women who were mourning and weeping

   • The soldiers who crucified him

• The thief who cried out to him for mercy

3. What contrasts do you see between the two thieves who were hanging on the crosses on each side of Jesus?

The First Cross: A Tragic Picture

An absolute tragedy occurred on the first cross we will examine. One of the criminals was hurling abuse and scorn at Jesus. During his last moments of life he was mocking, ridiculing, and spewing blasphemous things at the only One who could save him. Within hours of eternal judgment, he made a calculated decision to check out of this life with a fist clenched toward God. He was about to die in his sin, and this was the precise tragedy that Jesus came to avert at the cost of his own blood.

Throughout his earthly ministry Jesus taught this simple truth over and over again: "Whatever you do, whatever mistake you make, don't die in your sin." Why? Because the Word of God is sufficiently clear in its description of what happens to people who die in sin. The Scriptures tell us that those who die in sin end up standing before a holy, absolutely righteous God and must pay the price for those sins. Unforgiven sinners will be judged for their refusal to embrace Christ as their Savior; they will receive in eternity what they insisted on all throughout their life here on earth: separation from God. This means eternal condemnation and isolation from God — with no second chances.

This first cross paints a tragic picture because the unrepentant thief dies just inches from the touch of the Savior. The solution to his sin problem was right within his grasp and yet he chose to let it slip away. It happened two thousand years ago and this same tragedy repeats itself over and over again even today.

4. No one likes the idea of eternal judgment. The reality of hell is a topic many Christians ignore and avoid. As you read these passages, what are some of the sober realities the Bible teaches about hell?

5. How should the reality of eternal judgment impact the following?

• The way we live

• The way we interact with and pray for nonbelievers

• How we do church

6. Tell of a person you care about who is not yet a follower of Jesus Christ. How can your Christian friends pray for you and encourage you as you seek to let the love and light of God shine into this person's life?

The Second Cross: A Hope-Filled Picture

While we are mindful of the tragedy that occurred on one of the crosses next to Jesus, a radically different drama unfolded on the other side of the Savior. An unbelievable victory occurred just inches from Jesus. A man was forgiven from sin in the final hours of his life; it was an eleventh-hour rescue, a buzzer beater. This picture overflows with eternal hope!

Three distinct things happened in the final moments of this man's life:

- He admitted the truth about himself. He was a sinner and deserved the punishment he was facing.

- He acknowledged who Jesus was. Jesus had done no wrong. He saw Jesus for who he was — the Son of God!

- He cried out to Jesus. In his own clumsy way he said, "Remember me." This was his cry for salvation.

In his final moments this thief saw who he was, who Jesus was, and he turned to the only One who could wash him clean and change his eternal condition. What a powerful reminder that it is never too late, that we have never wandered too far away, that God's grace is always available.

Read Luke 23:32 – 43; Romans 10:9 – 11; and Acts 4:8 – 12

7. Some people can remember the exact day and moment they prayed to receive Jesus Christ as the leader of their life. Others can't remember an exact day but a season of life that their faith became real. All of us have a story about how we came to faith in Jesus. Briefly describe the journey that led you to embrace Jesus by faith and become his follower.

8. The thief who embraced Jesus gives a beautiful and simple picture of this journey. He saw himself as he was. He saw Jesus for who he was. And he cried out to Jesus for salvation. Why is each of these an important part of a spiritual journey:

- Seeing and acknowledging our spiritual poverty, sin, and need

• Acknowledging Jesus as the only One who can save and give new life

• Crying out to Jesus and asking for his salvation

How can these three things help inform and guide the way we reach out to people who are not yet followers of Jesus?

The Third Cross: A Picture of Grace

As we look at the three crosses silhouetted against the sky, three distinct stories unfold. The first is a tragedy. One man, so close to Jesus, ended up eternally separated from God. The second is a hope-filled story of redemption and forgiveness. A man on the brink of eternity embraced the Savior and entered paradise. The third cross, the one in the middle, is the most important story in human history. On this cross hung the gift of heaven: Jesus Christ.

On this cross the Lamb of God, the beautiful Savior, died for sin and sinners. He died on the cross *willingly*. He could have called on the angels of heaven to deliver him, but he was committed to pay the price for our sins and die in our place (Matthew 26:53). Jesus was emphatic that he laid down his life willingly (John 10:18). Jesus died *innocently*. He had never sinned, but he died to pay for our sins. Jesus also died *expectantly*. Through his grace-filled sacrifice Jesus knew that countless men, women, and children would be restored to relationship with the Father.

THE PASSION OF JESUS

Read John 3:16; 1 John 4:9 – 10; John 10:18; and Matthew 26:52 – 54

9. Much discussion and debate have surrounded who is to blame for Jesus' crucifixion. Some say it was the Roman government. Others point a finger at the Jewish leaders. If you could ask Jesus who was most responsible for him being on the cross, what do you think he would say?

10. The center cross silhouetted against the Jerusalem skyline is a picture of grace. How have you experienced and received grace because of Jesus' willing sacrifice on the cross?

11. Those who have experienced the grace of Jesus are called to be grace bearers in our world. How does a follower of Jesus bring grace into *one* of the following places of life?

- ☐ In a friendship with other believers
- ☐ In a friendship with nonbelievers
- ☐ In a marriage
- ☐ With children
- ☐ In the workplace
- ☐ In our neighborhood

Celebrating and Being Celebrated

One of the greatest sources of fuel for the uphill journey of life is grace. As we receive and experience God's grace, we are empowered to live for him. As we are amazed by grace, we are stirred to share it with others. Lift up prayers celebrating the grace of God and all it means to you:

- Jesus, thank you for your willingness to lay down your life for me.
- Father, I praise you for loving me enough to send your only Son.
- Spirit of God, I praise you for daily reminders of grace that you whisper in my ear.

Loving and Being Loved

We all have people we care about who are heading the same direction as the thief on the cross who mocked and rejected Jesus. It can be hard to know what to say or how to help these people. One of the best ways you can press forward is through prayer. Take time in the coming week to pray in some of the following directions:

Name of one person you are praying for: _____

- Pray for God to give you wisdom and grace as you interact with this person.
- Pray for the Holy Spirit to soften their heart to the love of God and the gospel.
- Ask for courage to share your story and how you came to know Jesus and embrace him as Savior.
- Pray against the devil's efforts to keep this person far from God.

Serving and Being Served

Identify a person in your life who is not yet a follower of Jesus. Contact them and let them know you have been thinking about them and just wanted to take them out for coffee or lunch (or offer some kind of service that you know would be meaningful to them). Be sure you are really ready to step up and extend grace-filled service. You never know what they might ask of you. As you serve, pray that the reality of God's grace will flow through this act of ministry.

The Ultimate Sacrifice

LUKE 23:26 – 49

ATONEMENT. IMAGINE RECEIVING A SPEEDING TICKET FOR DRIVING 75 MPH IN a 55 mph zone. You know you are guilty because your eyes darted down to your speedometer the second you heard the siren and noticed the flashing lights in your rearview mirror. You are declared guilty of speeding and are given a ticket that reminds you that you must atone for your moving violation in order to satisfy the demands of the court justice system. Within thirty days you are expected to shell out the amount of money designated.

If you pay your fine (or, if your state allows, attend an optional traffic safety class), you will have atoned for your crime. You will have satisfied the demands of justice and can go back about your business confident that the issue is settled. That's the idea of atonement: satisfying the demands of justice to ensure that a crime that has been committed is paid for in full.

Substitute. When you were in elementary school and your regular teacher was sick, the school would assign a substitute to cover the class. Their role was to stand in the place of the educator who was normally there and take care of the class for the day. We all understand the idea of a substitute. Substitution is about someone taking the place of another person. It is one person standing in and doing the job of another.

Substitutionary Atonement. When these two words are put together, we have a rich and important concept that represents what Jesus did on his uphill walk to the cross. Substitutionary atonement is the idea that Jesus paid the price for our sins when he died in our place on the cross. He was our substitute and he atoned for our wrongs.

This theme weaves through the pages of the Bible from Genesis to Revelation. When Adam and Eve sinned and disobeyed God by eating the forbidden fruit, God covered their shame with the skin of an animal that had to die to provide clothing.

When God was about to free his people from bondage in Egypt, an innocent lamb's blood was put on the doorposts of the Israelites' homes. The presence of this blood caused the angel of death to pass over these homes, and they experienced no judgment.

In Israel's God-given tradition, there was a yearly celebration of the Day of Atonement. On this day the sins of the nation were symbolically placed on an innocent sacrificial animal that bore them away.

When John the Baptist saw Jesus approach him for baptism at the Jordan River, he declared, "Look, the Lamb of God, who takes away the sin of the world!" (John 1:29). All through the Bible we see this picture of a substitutionary sacrifice that cleanses us from sin.

Making the Connection

1. Tell about a moment in your spiritual journey when you became profoundly aware that Jesus did more than pay for sins; he paid for *your* sins, took *your* punishment, and died in *your* place.

Knowing and Being Known

Read Exodus 12:21 – 23; Isaiah 53:5 – 7; John 1:29 – 31; 1 Peter 3:18; and Hebrews 9:24 – 28

2. What are some of the connections between the Old Testament sacrifices and the death of Jesus on the cross?

3. What do we mean when we say, "Jesus atones for our sins"?

What do we mean when we say, "Jesus died in our place, as our substitute"?

A Final Day of Atonement

There will come a final day in redemptive history. It could be called a day of reckoning, or a final Day of Atonement. The Bible teaches that each of us is going to stand before our holy God and give a reckoning or account for our life. On this day the demands of God's holiness will be met. The gavel of divine justice will be struck one final time.

It is important that we understand with crystal clarity what will happen on this day. We will *not* be asked, "Did you sin?" Our sins have already been recorded. Our lies, thefts, lusts, exaggerations, profanity, explosions of anger, dishonesty, gossip, and countless other transgressions are all part of the moral record. The issue will not be: did you sin? It will be: who is going to pay for your sins?

Read Romans 3:21 – 26 and Hebrews 10:10 – 14

4. Using Scripture, how would you respond to a person who makes *one* of the following statements?

☐ I have lived a pretty good life. If I had to stand before God and give an account for how I have lived, I think I would fare pretty well.

☐ I don't need someone else to take care of my wrongs. I want to be responsible and pay for them myself.

☐ I might have done a few wrong things, but my "sins" are nothing compared to people who have committed murder and other really big sins.

5. People have all kinds of hypotheses about how things will play out when they stand before God. For instance, some people picture huge scales in heaven. God will place all their good deeds on one side and their wrongs on the other. If the scales tip toward the good side, they get into heaven. If they tip the wrong way, they could be in trouble. What are some of the other judgment day theories floating around?

Self-Atonement

When it comes to atonement for our sins, there are really only two options. The first is that we can atone for our own sins. We can satisfy the demands of justice, pay the price ourselves. A lot of people make this choice. They have an awareness of who Jesus was and what he did. They have heard the message but, sadly, they say, "You know what? I don't want it. I don't need God. I don't want Jesus. I'll take my own hit at the end of time." They have no idea what they're saying. When that hit comes, it's going to be beyond their worst nightmare. It's going to be the single most intense moment of regret that any human being ever faces. In that moment they'll realize self-atonement is a terrible idea. They'll realize the hit they're taking: separation from God forever.

God doesn't want anybody to self-atone. From the garden of Eden forward, God has been providing a substitutionary atonement — from an innocent animal in the garden to lambs in the sacrificial system to a scapegoat and a sacrificial goat on the Day of Atonement. Finally he provided Jesus, his own Son, the Lamb of God, so that nobody would have to self-atone on the final day. But some people make their choice and say they don't want Jesus. When this happens God lets them have their own way, and they are left with an eternity apart from him.

Read John 3:17 – 21

6. What leads some people to feel the need to self-atone and not rely on Jesus?

7. What does the Bible teach will happen to those who refuse the grace of Jesus and rely on their own life and good works for salvation?

8. What would you say to a person who is nearing the end of life and still has not received the substitutionary atonement offered through faith in Jesus Christ?

Substitutionary Atonement

The wisest choice any human being could make in this life is to accept the grace of God revealed in Jesus Christ. When they do, the substitutionary atonement of Jesus covers their sins, washes them clean, and gives new life. Jesus is the only One who can do this. These are the options: let Jesus pay the price or pay it yourself.

We live in a day of tremendous religious diversity. Some people want to give equal weight and validity to all religious expressions. The Bible does not leave room for this. No other religious leader can atone for our sins. Mohammed did not die a substitutionary atoning death; he just died. Confucius, Buddha, other religious figureheads through history can't pay for sins and wash anyone clean. They didn't lead anybody to believe that their death was an atoning sacrifice. Only Jesus truly saves.

Read John 14:6; Acts 4:8 – 12; and John 3:16

9. In a day when media and culture embrace any religious expression as equally valid, how do these passages paint a dramatically different picture of salvation?

10. How would you respond to *one* of the following?

    ☐ A nonbeliever who says: "You Christians are just too narrow in your thinking. It would be more loving to accept other religions as optional paths to God."

    ☐ A nonbeliever who says: "The Bible does not make exclusive claims that Jesus is the only way to God. That's just the teaching of closed-minded church people."

    ☐ A Christian who says: "It is not our place to bother other people with our beliefs. If someone with a devout faith is not Christian, we should just leave them alone."

    ☐ A Christian who says: "Jesus is my way to God, but there are certainly many other ways. Who are we to claim Jesus is the only way?"

11. What are some natural ways we can share the message of Jesus' substitutionary atonement with people we love who are not followers of Jesus?

    How can your family members and Christian friends encourage you and pray for you as you seek to tell the story of salvation that is found in Jesus alone?

Celebrating and Being Celebrated

God could have left us in our sin. He could have offered only one option: self-atonement. But in his amazing grace and love, he made a way. He offered his only Son, Jesus, as the sacrificial lamb to pay the price for us. As you close this study, thank God for this indescribable gift, using any of the following prayer starters:

- Father, thank you for loving us enough to offer your beloved Son as the sacrifice for our sins.
- Jesus, I praise you for going to the cross willingly and taking the uphill journey for me.
- God, you have made a way to deliver us from our sins and the judgment we deserve—I give you praise.

Loving and Being Loved

Real people will spend eternity in a real heaven or a real hell. All of us have friends or family members who are still in a place of choosing self-atonement. If they do not accept God's offer of atonement through Jesus Christ, the consequences are more serious than anyone can imagine. As an act of love, commit to tell one person about how much Jesus means to you. Share your story of coming to faith in Jesus. Also, offer to tell the story of God's love and the sacrifice of Jesus with this person. If you are not sure how to tell your story of faith, consider one of these helpful books: *Just Walk Across the Room*, by Bill Hybels, or *Organic Outreach for Ordinary People*: *Sharing Good News Naturally*, by Kevin Harney.

Serving and Being Served

One of the ways we can open the door to share spiritual things with others is by revealing the grace of Jesus through humble service. Jesus touched and healed lepers, ministered to the hurting, fed the hungry, and offered many acts of service. As people saw his love and care, they were willing to listen to his teaching.

Identify one person in your life who has not yet entered a life-saving relationship with Jesus and find one way to serve them in the coming week. As you serve them, pray for an open door to share your journey of faith and the message of Jesus with them.

Wiser Together
DVD Study

Learning to Live the Right Way

Bill Hybels

with Shane Farmer and Todd Katter

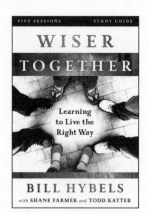

In this five-session video-based Bible study (study guide and video sold separately), bestselling author and pastor Bill Hybels challenges you to make doing life together a priority, exploring from the book of Proverbs how experiencing community and growing in wisdom are inseparably linked and offering practical direction on how to experience this with others.

All of us want to get better at life. Getting wiser alone, however, is not the way it works. God didn't wire us to catch onto wise and godly living through lone-ranger attempts at learning; it's something that rubs off on us when we spend time with others who have the wisdom of God living inside of them. As the proverb says, "Iron sharpens iron as one person sharpens another."

This study is designed with both new and experienced group leaders in mind. For new leaders, it includes optional weekly DVD training sessions to help them lead a fantastic, first-time small group experience. For experienced leaders, it includes a "Going Deeper" section for those ready to take this content to the next level.

Sessions include:

1. Walking with the Wise
2. The Counsel of Community
3. Iron Sharpens Iron
4. The Heart of Community
5. Faith and Friendship

Available in stores and online!

Too Busy Not to Pray DVD Study

Slowing Down to Be with God

Bill Hybels with Ashley Wiersma

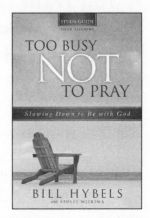

Bestselling author and pastor Bill Hybels offers timeless concepts based on his book of the same name that has sold over one million copies, helping individuals and small groups develop an understanding and enjoyment of prayer.

The urgent need for prayer in today's broken world is clear, but busyness still keeps many of us from finding time to pray. So Bill Hybels offers us his practical, time-tested ideas on praying effectively.

In this four-session video Bible study based on his classic book on prayer, *Too Busy Not to Pray,* Bill Hybels calls us to make prayer a priority, broadening the vision for what our eternal, powerful God does when his people slow down to pray.

The coordinating study guide (sold separately) leads individuals and small groups through discussion topics, group activities, and in-between-studies assignments.

The session titles include:

1. Why Pray?
2. Our Part of the Deal
3. When Prayer Feels Hard
4. People of Prayer

Hybels helps you listen to God and learn how to respond. As a result, you will grow closer to God and experience the benefits of spending time with him.

Available in stores and online!

If You Want to Walk on Water, You've Got to Get Out of the Boat DVD Study

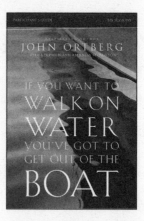

John Ortberg
with Stephen and Amanda Sorenson

Peter may have been the first one out of the boat, but Jesus' invitation to walk on water is for you as well. But walk on water? What does that mean?

In this six-session small group Bible study (participant's guide and DVD sold separately), you'll learn how to move beyond fear to discover God's unique calling for your life! *If You Want to Walk on Water, You've Got to Get Out of the Boat* helps you answer helps you answer Christ's call to greater faith, power-filled deeds, and a new way of knowing how to discern God's call, transcend fear, risk faith, manage failure, and trust God. Relating the story in Matthew 14 to life today, teacher and bestselling author John Ortberg invites you to consider the incredible potential that awaits you outside your comfort zone.

Sessions include:

1. What's Water Walking?
2. The Tragedy of the Unopened Gift
3. Find Your Calling and Get Your Feet Wet!
4. Facing Our Challenges, Conquering Our Fears
5. Good News for Cave Dwellers
6. Learning to Wait on Our Big God

Available in stores and online!

God Is Closer Than You Think DVD Study

John Ortberg

with Stephen and Amanda Sorenson

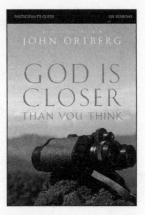

Intimacy with God can happen right now ... a closeness you can feel, a reality you can experience for yourself. God is closer than you think, and connecting with him isn't the exclusive domain of monks and ascetics. It's for business people, high school students, busy moms, single men, single women ... and most important, it's for YOU!

In this six-session video-based Bible study (participant's guide and DVD sold separately), John Ortberg reveals the face of God waiting to be discovered in the complex mosaic of your life. This insightful and impactful small group study will help you:

- Find God where you least expect him
- Listen to God's voice
- Identify which pathway of relationship you're uniquely designed to travel
- Align yourself with the flow of the Holy Spirit
- Draw closer to God even when he seems absent

Sessions include:

1. God's Great Desire for People
2. Where Is God in My World?
3. Partnering with God Today
4. Listening to the Voice of God
5. God Wants a Relationship with You
6. Heaven Breaking Through

Available in stores and online!

WILLOW CREEK ASSOCIATION

This resource is just one of many ministry tools published in partnership with the Willow Creek Association. Founded in 1992, WCA was created to serve churches and church leaders striving to create environments where those still outside the family of God are welcomed—and can more easily consider God's loving offer of salvation through faith.

These innovative churches and leaders are connected at the deepest level by their all-out dedication to Christ and His Kingdom. Willing to do whatever it required to build churches that help people move along the path toward Christ-centered devotion; they also share a deep desire to encourage all believers at every step of their faith journey, to continue moving toward a fully transformed, Christ-centered life.

Today, more than 10,000 churches from 80 denominations worldwide are formally connected to WCA and each other through WCA Membership. Many thousands more come to WCA for networking, training, and resources.

For more information about the ministry of the
Willow Creek Association, visit: **willowcreek.com**.